Medieval Philosophical Texts in Translation

No. 30

Roland J. Teske, S.J., Editor

Lee C. Rice, Associate Editor

William of Auvergne

THE IMMORTALITY OF THE SOUL

[De immortalitate animae]

Translated from the Latin
With an Introduction and Notes

by

Roland J. Teske, S.J.

Marquette University Press

Milwaukee, Wisconsin

Printed in the United States of America
ISBN 0-87462-233-6
Library of Congress Catalogue Card Number: 91-75282

Fratribus meis

Societatis Jesu

Table of Contents

Abbreviations

AHDLMA	*Archives d'histoire doctrinale et littéraire du moyen âge*
BA	*Bibliothèque Augustinienne*
CC	*Corpus Christianorum*
MS	*Mediaeval Studies*
PL	*Patrologia Latina*
SC	*Sources Chrétiennes*
TMS	*The Modern Schoolman*

Introduction

1. The Question of Authorship

Before one can date *De immortalitate animae*, one must face the question of its authorship. One version of the work has been attributed to Dominicus Gundissalinus, and a slightly different version has been attributed to William of Auvergne. Though the contemporary scholarly judgment now attributes both versions of the work to William, an introduction to the question must say something about Gundissalinus, who had for a long time been considered its author.

Dominicus Gundissalinus (Dominic Gundisalvi) was a twelfth century cleric and scholar who is principally known as the translator of various works of Arabian philosophy, though he is also the author of several works of his own. He was an archdeacon of the diocese of Segovia; yet he spent much of his life in Toledo. In collaboration with either Ibn Daoud (Avendeath) or John of Spain, he translated Avicenna's *De anima, Metaphysics* and a part of his *Posterior Analytics*, as well as the *Metaphysics* of Algazel and the *Fons vitae* of Ibn Gabirol (Avicebron). Gundisalvi's own works include *The Division of Philosophy* (*De divisione philosophiae*), which was written about 1150, *The Procession of the World* (*De processione mundi*), *Unity* (*De unitate*), and *The Soul* (*De anima*).[1] *The Immortality of the Soul* has, of course, also been attributed to him, though the evidence now indicates, as I shall show, that William of Auvergne is its author.[2] According to Aubert, Gundissalinus's significance lies in the fact that he introduced to the West "the mixture of Neoplatonic and Aristotelian philosophy developed in the Arab world" and thus was "one of the artisans of what E. Gilson has called 'Avicennizing Augustinism'."[3] Gundissalinus died sometime after 1190.

---

1. The *De divisione philosophiae* was edited by L. Baur in *Beiträge zur Geschichte der Philosophie des Mittelalters* IV 2/3 (Münster: Aschendorff, 1903). The *De processione mundi* was edited by G. Bülow in *Beiträge* XXIV 3 (1925). The *De unitate* was edited by P. Correns in *Beiträge* I 1 (1891). The *De anima* was edited by J. T. Muckle in *MS* II (1949) 23-103.

2. G. Bülow edited the *De immortalitate animae* in: *Des Dominicus Gundissalinus Schrift von der Unsterblichkeit der Seele, nebst einem Anhange, enthaltend die Abhandlung des Wilhelm von Paris "De immortalitate animae,"* in *Beiträge* II 3 (Münster: Aschendorff, 1897).

3. Cf. "Gundissalvi (Dominique), Gundissalinus, Gondisalvi," by R. Aubert, in *Dictionnaire d'histoire et de géographie ecclésiastique.* Vol. 22 (Paris: Letouzey et Ané, 1988), pp. 1168-1170, here p. 1169.

In a note that summarizes the history of the question of the authorship of *De immortalitate animae*, Baudoin Allard points out that in 1898 Clemens Baeumker attributed the treatise to Gundissalinus.[4] In the previous year, 1897, Georg Bülow edited the two almost identical treatises.[5] Bülow attributed the *De immortalitate* to Gundissalinus, while trying to exonerate William of the charge of plagiarism. Bülow viewed William's work as a youthful scholarly exercise that, he says, William would have had no intention to claim as his own work. Nonetheless, Bülow acknowledges that William went on to make use of his copy of the work, to which he had made various additions, as though it were his own work and without any worry as to whether what he used was really his own or belonged to Gundissalinus. Bülow suggests that William either had a deficient sense of literary property or simply forgot the extent of his borrowing from Gundissalinus.[6] Moreover, Bülow claims that the Middle Ages lacked a sense of literary property and turned a blind eye to the near identity of the two texts, though he is unwilling to affirm this supposition as more than probable.[7] M. de Wulf, on the other hand, accused William of plagiarism pure and simple.[8]

In 1945-46 Amato Masnovo rejected Bülow's conclusion, pointing out that of the manuscripts that Bülow used to establish the text of Gundissalinus's *De immortalitate animae*, only one, dating from the second half of the 13th century, was expressly attributed to him, while the others were anonymous.[9] Furthermore, Masnovo pointed out that William attributed to himself a treatise on the immortality of the soul, that antedated his *De anima*.[10] He also argued that William's *De anima*, in

---

4. "Dominicus Gundissalinus als philosophischer Schriftsteller," *Compte rendu du 4e Congrès scientifique international des catholiques* IIIe Section, Freibourg, Switzerland, 1898, pp. 50f; cited from B. Allard, "Une note sur le 'De immortalitate animae' de Guillaume d'Auvergne," *Bulletin de philosophie médiévale* 18 (1976) 68-72; here 69.

5. Cf. Bülow, note 2 above.

6. "Wilhelm hat, und zwar in seinen jüngeren Jarhren, die Abhandlung des Dominicus 'De immortalitate animae' zum Zwecke des Selbststudiums durchgearbeitet und wahrscheinlich für seinem Privatgebrauch abgeschrieben. Hierbei hat er an der selben eine Reihe von Anderungen vorgenommen, die nach seinem subjectiven Ermessen die Brauchbarkeit des Buches erhöhten. In späteren Jahren hat er dann diese Uberarbeitung und die in ihr enthaltenen philosophischen Gedanken gelegentlich der Abfassung anderer Schriften mehrfach benutzt. Hierbei hat er sich dann die Schrift 'De immortalitate animae' selbst zugeschrieben, sei es infolge des mangelhaften Begriffes vom literarischen Eigentum, sei es, weil er in der Tat nach Verlauf der Jahre(n) nicht mehr wusste, wieviel von jener Schrift anderswo entlehnt und wieviel sein geistiges Eigentum sei" (Bülow, p. 98). Cf. also Baudoin C. Allard, "Note sur le *De immortalitate animae*," p. 69.

7. Bülow, p. 99.

8. Cf. M. de Wulf, *Histoire de la philosophie médiévale* VI,2: *Le treizième siècle* (Louvain and Paris, 1936), p. 66.

9. A. Masnovo, *Da Guglielmo d'Auvergne a san Tommaso d'Aquino* (Milan: Vita et Pensiero, 1945-1946), III, pp. 119-123.

10. As evidence of this Masnovo cites William's *De anima* twice: ch. I, pt. 6 (II, 72a) and ch. V, pt. 22 (II, 147a); cf. Masnovo, p. 120.

dealing with the immortality of the soul, reflects on so many points of language and content the *De immortalitate* that, if the *De immortalitate* is the work of Gundissalinus, it is hardly possible to attribute to William even the *De anima* as an original work.[11]

Furthermore, Masnovo finds the supposed lack of a sense of literary property in the Middle Ages is exaggerated. He argues that it would not require a terribly delicate conscience on the part of a medieval man, not merely a priest, but the bishop of Paris, to recognize the wrongness of attributing another's book to himself, and yet William of Auvergne attributes to himself in his *De anima* the *De immortalitate animae* that Bülow attributes to Gundissalinus.[12] Rather than suppose that the fault lies with William's failure to remember, Masnovo suggests that the faulty memory or distractedness might lie with a scribe. Moreover, Masnovo points out that for establishing the text of the work Bülow attributed to Gundissalinus, Bülow used not merely the Paris manuscript (P) which contains the attribution to Gundissalinus and lacks the additions found in B, the Brussels manuscript containing the version he attributes to William, but also C, a manuscript from Chartres, which also lacks these additions.[13] Masnovo notes that the scribe of the manuscript P, dating from the second half of the 13th century, is the first to speak of a *De immortalitate animae* of Gundissalinus. Neither Albert the Great nor Robert Grosseteste refer to a *De immortalitate animae* of Gundissalinus. Philip the Chancellor may have cited the *De immortalitate animae* in the first half of the century, but he does not mention Gundissalinus. In any case Masnovo argues that it is plausible to suppose that the chancellor was alluding to a work by his own bishop.[14]

Masnovo also argues that Gundissalinus, the translator of Avicebron's *Fons vitae*, seems to have adopted the latter's doctrine of universal hylomorphism, which is not found in *De immortalitate animae* or in William's works. Hence, Bülow, who places the *De immortalitate* after the translation of *Fons vitae*, is forced to suppose that Gundissalinus first adopted and then abandoned universal hylomorphism. For such reasons, Masnovo came to doubt the authenticity of the *De immortalitate animae* of Gundissalinus and to hold that there were two nearly identical versions of the text, both due to William of Auvergne, the latter written after his *De anima*.[15]

---

11. Masnovo, p. 120. In the footnotes to the translation I shall illustrate the correctness of this claim by extensive citations from parallel passages in William's *De anima*.

12. Masnovo, p. 121; cf. note 10 above.

13. Masnovo, p. 121.

14. Masnovo, p. 122.

15. Masnovo, pp. 122-123; Allard, "Note sur le *De immortalitate animae*," p. 70.

Despite the arguments of Masnovo, such an outstanding histo-
rian of medieval philosophy as Etienne Gilson said in referring to Bülow's
volume, "This work contains the text of *Gundissalinus de immortalitate
animae*, pp. 1-38; in comparing the two texts, one sees that William's is a
plagiarism of that of Gundissalinus."[16]

Allard points out that Bülow used none of the three manuscripts
in which the *De immortalitate animae* was explicitly attributed to
William – manuscripts that had been noted by Noël Valois as early as
1880.[17] Furthermore, Allard reports that he has discovered six more
manuscripts. Of the six that Allard has discovered, only one is
anonymous, while the others are explicitly attributed to William,
"although in four of the five cases the *Incipit* is that of the text attributed
by Baeumker to Gundissalinus."[18] Hence, Allard claims that nearly the
whole manuscript tradition, as well as ancient and modern authors,
attributes the *De immortalitate animae* to William of Auvergne.[19] While
Gilson accuses William of plagiarizing the work of Gundissalinus, Allard
suggests that the work attributed to Gundissalinus should be viewed as
William's. A definitive solution to the question of the authorship of the *De
immortalitate* will have to await the new editions of the *De anima* and the
De immortalitate promised by Allard some fifteen years ago.[20] In the
meanwhile it seems safe to say that the weight of scholarly opinion and of
the evidence favors the view that regards William of Auvergne as the
author of *De immortalitate animae* rather than Gundissalinus.[21] If William
is taken as its author, then it seems plausible to date one version as
relatively early in William's career, probably before 1228, and the second
version somewhat later either before or after the *De anima* which was
most likely written around 1235.[22]

---

16. "Avicenne en occident au moyen age," *AHDLMA* 44 (1969) 101-102, n. 12; my
translation.

17. Allard, "Note sur le *De immortalitate animae*," p. 70.

18. B. Allard, "Nouvelles additions et corrections au *Répertoire* de Glorieux: à propos de
Guillaume d'Auvergne," *Bulletin de philosophie médiévale* 10-12 (1968-70) 79-80.

19. Allard, "Note sur le *De immortalitate animae*," p. 71.

20. Allard, "Note sur le *De immortalitate animae*," p. 69.

21. In an article that summarizes the contemporary scholarly judgment on the matter,
Gabriel Jüssen reports, "Allard hat, im Folge von Masnovo, gegen Bülow und den
Konsensus der Forschung starke Gründe dafür vorgebracht, dass der in Bülows Edition
Dominikus Gundissalinus zugeschriebene Traktat *De immortalitate animae*, die
angenommene Vorlage für Wilhelms gleichnamiges Werk, in Wirklichkeit auch dem
Auvergnaten zugehört, so dass dann beide Traktate als (engste) Varianten ein und
desselben Werks aufzufassen wären." G. Jüssen, "Wilhelm von Auvergne," in
Contemporary Philosophy. A New Survey. Volume 6: Philosophy and Science in the Middle
Ages. Part 1 (Dordrecht: Kluwer Academic Publishers, 1990), pp. 177-185, here p. 177.

22. Cf. Allard, "Note sur le *De immortalitate animae*," p. 72. For the dating of the various
works of William, cf. Josef Kramp, "Des Wilhelm von Auvergne 'Magisterium Divinale',"
Gregorianum 1 (1920) 538-613, 2 (1921) 42-103 and 174-195.

2. The Author and his Works

William of Auvergne was born in Aurillac in the Province of Auvergne, perhaps as early as 1180 or as late as 1190.[23] Little is known of his early life, though by 1223 he was a canon of Notre Dame and a master of theology at the University of Paris. In 1228 Gregory IX named him the new bishop of Paris. During his early years as bishop the masters and students of the University went on strike over the violation of their rights and withdrew from Paris to neighboring cities. When William failed to secure the settlement of the strike, Gregory accused him of destroying the university and expressed his regret over ordaining him bishop. In the long run, the strike, which was soon settled, had good results insofar as it contributed to withdrawing the university from the control of the local bishop. William was also instrumental in bringing the first masters from the Franciscans and Dominicans to the University of Paris. William presided over the diocese of Paris until his death in 1249.

William's principal work is the multi-volume *Teaching on God in the Mode of Wisdom* (*Magisterium divinale et sapientiale*). Until the time of Kramp's articles early in this century, the individual parts were not seen as constituting one immense work. The principal parts of the *Magisterium divinale* are the following: *The Trinity* (*De trinitate*), *The Universe of Creatures* (*De universo creaturarum*), *The Soul* (*De anima*), *The Reasons Why God Became Man* (*De causis cur Deus homo*), *Faith and Laws* (*De fide et de legibus*), *The Sacraments* (*De sacramentis*), and *Virtues and Morals* (*De virtutibus et de moribus*). William's other works include: *Divine Rhetoric* (*De rhetorica divina*) and two treatises entitled *Good and Evil* (*De bono et malo*).

William is one of the first philosopher-theologians of the thirteenth century to grapple seriously with the influx of Greek and Arabian philosophical thought that poured into the West during the latter half of the twelfth and first part of the thirteenth century. Despite ecclesiastical warnings against and condemnations of Aristotelian thought, the bishop of Paris obviously continued to read and absorb into his own thought many features of the worldview of Aristotle and his followers. William was especially influenced by the philosophy of Avicenna and yet retained a critical stance toward the Peripatetics wherever he found them in conflict with the Christian faith.[24] He was one of the first to understand that philosophical errors had to be met with philosophical argumentation and

---

23. For William's life, cf. Noël Valois, *Guillaume d'Auvergne évêque de Paris (1228-1249): sa vie et ses ouvrages* (Paris: Picard, 1880), as well as the introduction to *The Trinity*, pp. 1-5.

24. In *De anima* ch. II, pt. 12 (II, 82b), William says of Aristotle, "Although in many matters we have to contradict Aristotle, as is truly right and proper, and this holds for all those statements by which he contradicts the truth, still he should be accepted, that is, upheld, in all those statements in which he is found to have held the correct position."

that a metaphysics like that of Avicenna's offered on many points the possibility of a more profound articulation of the Christian view of God, man and the world.

3. The Content of the Work

William begins by pointing out four or, in the later version, five ways in which human errors are remedied: sensation, punishment, philosophy, authority, and revelation. William claims that error regarding the natural immortality of the human soul is destructive of the very foundation of morality and religion. He is thoroughly convinced that one who lacks a belief in the soul's immortality will surrender to every vice and regard any exhortation to moral goodness as an attempt to deceive the ignorant. He warns that human affairs will be intolerably disturbed, that life and morals will be confused, and that the Creator will be dishonored.

In his mercy, then, God has provided remedies for this error: law and its penalties for the contemptuous, philosophy with its proofs for those who lack knowledge, prophecy and revelation for those who accept the Scriptures, the testimony of those raised from the dead, and, finally, the experience of souls who withdraw from external things into themselves for those who are willing to enter into themselves.

In this work William sets out to show how philosophy confronts the erroneous belief that our souls are mortal. He omits the authorities of the Scriptures and of the early saints, as well as the experiences recorded in such works as *The Dialogues* of Gregory the Great, realizing that such arguments will not prevail over the arguments of the philosophers against whom he is arguing. William mentions that he will use the authority and arguments of Aristotle who deals with this question in *On the Soul*, referring vaguely to the second book.[25]

William begins with a set of arguments based upon attributes of God, such as divine goodness, justice, and wisdom. He recalls for his reader that a syllogistic argument should have premises drawn from the proper subject matter if it is to be demonstrative. Nonetheless, he permits arguments with premises drawn from extraneous grounds because of human ignorance coupled with the desire to know the truth. He also points to the precedent set by St. Peter who appealed to the justice of God in arguing with Simon Magus in what we now call pseudo-Clementine literature in order to show the existence of the next life. In his *De anima* William sets forth a longer series of such proofs based on God

---

25. Cf. translation, p. 25.

in the mode of wisdom (*per vias probationum sapientialium et divinalium*) which often closely parallel the arguments of the *De immortalitate animae*).[26]

Then William turns to a series of proofs based on "proper" grounds, that is, upon the nature of the soul and its activities. Though the structure of this part of the work is not always clear, especially in the central section which is found early in the version Bülow attributed to Gundissalinus and later in the version he attributed to William, there are five or six distinct arguments. William explicitly points out the first two "root principles" or major premises which he attributes to Aristotle.[27] The third argument builds upon two root principles, namely, that "no motion of nature is pointless" and that "nothing that is moved naturally is kept by a natural necessity from the end toward which it is moved."[28] The fourth argument is less clearly delineated. Either it is expressed in the form of an enthymeme, or it is to be taken as part of what I have labelled the fifth argument.[29] The latter argument appeals to the four possible ways in which something can be destroyed and argues that the human soul cannot be destroyed in any of these ways. William lists as possible ways in which something can be destroyed: the separation of form and matter, the separation of integral parts, the destruction of the sustaining subject, and the removal of the efficient cause.[30] He excludes a fifth manner of destruction, namely, the tendency of anything created to fall back into non-being. William clearly argues to exclude the first, second and fourth modes of destruction from the soul; however, it is not clear where he argues to exclude the third mode of destruction, though he mentions that he has already done so when he turns to the fourth mode of destruction.[31] Since the third mode of destruction, that is, by the destruction of that which bears or sustains the soul, would have to meet the objection that the soul is destroyed by the destruction of the body or depends upon it for its continued existence, one can take the section of the translation found on pages 40 to 47, that is, the section found later in the version attributed to William by Bülow, as William's exclusion of the soul's destructibility by

---

26. Cf. *De anima* ch. VI, pt. 22 (II, 176b); cf. translation, note 11.

27. Cf. translation, p. 27 and p. 31, where William states the "root principles," and p. 33, where he attributes the arguments to "Aristotle and his followers."

28. Cf. translation, p. 34. William also states the second root principle in positive form: "it is naturally possible to attain everything that is naturally desired" (p. 35).

29. Bülow distinguishes what I have called the fourth argument into two. He labels one as "variations on the previous proof." The other argues that the position of the human soul between pure spirits and animal and vegetative souls indicates that some parts of the human soul are mortal, while others, including the soul itself, are immortal. Whatever is the case, William does not clearly differentiate the structure of the argumentation in this middle section.

30. Cf. translation, p. 46.

31. Cf. translation, p. 51; cf. also p. 47, where he also mentions the third mode of destruction.

reason of the destruction of the body. If that interpretation is correct, then what I have called the fourth argument is better taken as a part of the fifth.[32] The sixth argument rests upon the comparison of sensation and intellection.[33]

In each of these arguments, William clearly signals the minor premises by an initial "moreover" and generally introduces objections with "if someone should say." Thus one root principle or major premise is often followed by a series of arguments developing the minor premises of an argument. In any case, such stylistic devices render the *De immortalitate animae* far more like William's *The Trinity* than Gundissalinus's *De anima*.[34]

Rather than provide a detailed narrative description of the development of the argumentation, I offer an outline of the treatise. For comments on the sources of various arguments and their interpretation, see the footnotes to the translation.

4. An Outline of the Work

I. The Introduction

1. Divine goodness has provided four or five remedies for human errors.

2. The error about the soul's mortality leads to serious evils.

3. How the various divine remedies heal this error.

II. The Body of the Text

The goal of the present work is to show how the authority and arguments of philosophy deal with this error, while leaving aside the authorities of the Scriptures and the Fathers.

---

32. Perhaps one might also argue on these grounds for the preferability of the order of the text that is found in the version attributed to William.

33. Cf. translation, p. 52.

34. Cf. Gilson, "Avicenne en occident au moyen âge," p. 102, n. 12, where Gilson says of *De immortalitate animae*, "The style of the treatise of Gundissalinus is naturally that of his own Latin translations of Avicenna . . . ." However, Gundissalinus's *De anima* bears much less resemblance in terms of style to the Latin of Avicenna than does William's *De trinitate* or the *De immortalitate animae*.

A. Arguments based upon the nature of God.

Human ignorance along with the desire for knowledge leads us to use arguments that are less than demonstrative.

1. If God does not in the life to come reward those who serve him in this life, he is either lacking in wisdom or in goodness.

2. The justice of God requires that the good be rewarded and the bad be punished after this life.

3. Perfect justice demands that there be a judgment after this life.

4. Divine wisdom has counseled us to disdain the goods of the present life and would have misled us if the good are not rewarded and the bad punished hereafter.

B. Arguments based on the nature and activities of the soul.

1. If the activity of a substance does not depend upon the body, its essence does not depend upon the body. But the activity of the intellect does not depend upon the body.

Because the intellect's proper activity is not impeded by the body.

Because the intellect is most vigorous when the body is weakened by age.

Because, unlike mortal things, the intellective power is not weakened by age.

Objection: The intellective power is impeded or weakened when the body is impeded or weakened. William distinguishes between being injured by and being occupied with bodily disturbances.

Because the activity of the intellective power is invigorated and strengthened in separation from the body, e.g., in ecstasy and rapture.

2. Every substance, whose form is incorruptible, is itself incorruptible. But every intelligent substance is such, because it has no material forms as its own.

Because the intellect receives the likenesses of all forms.

Because there is no contrariety or opposition in immaterial things.

Objection: The animal soul is also an immaterial form. William distinguishes two sorts of material forms and points out that the animal soul is not receptive of all forms.

Objection: There can be an immaterial corruption if there is immaterial pain. William distinguishes two senses of pain and loss.

[These arguments are taken from Aristotle; those from Plato are passed over as inconclusive.]

3. No natural motion is pointless or in vain, and there are spiritual as well as bodily motions.

Objection: All motion is bodily. William stipulates that motion is merely taken as the way of attaining or avoiding something.

Every natural desire aims at something naturally possible; it is naturally possible to attain whatever is naturally desired. But the human soul has a natural desire for true and integral happiness and a natural aversion for true misery. Hence, there must be true spiritual happiness.

Because no power can be made happy save through its proper goods.

Because bodily things subject their lovers to unhappiness.

Because a love for lower things subjects the soul to them.

Because a spiritual power must have its own objects of apprehension, just as the sensible powers do.

Because the intellective power would have no nobility, if it had only temporal and transitory things as its objects.

Because the perfection of this power must be proportionate to its nature.

Because the perfection of this power, as its activity, has its perfection apart from the body.

Hence, the evasion of its misery and attainment of its happiness is naturally possible for the intellective power.

The permanence of the soul is not caused by happiness, but is a disposition that precedes it.

4. The life of the intellective power is not dependent upon the body.

Because rapture and application to more noble intelligible objects are neither violent nor a matter of chance, but either natural or voluntary.

Because the intellective power has two faces and can turn to its higher or lower objects.

Because a powerful object of the intellect leaves the intellect strengthened rather than weakened.

Because the intellect does not have a bodily organ. Though it is prevented from reading the book of the sensible world through an injury to the middle brain, it is still able to read its more noble book.

5. What is destructible can be destroyed only in four ways:

i) by the division of form from matter, either with the form remaining or without the form remaining.

ii) by the division of integral parts.

iii) by the destruction of what sustains or bears it.

iv) by the removal of its cause.

There is no fifth mode of destruction that is not reducible to one of these.

The human soul cannot be destroyed in the first manner, since it is pure form and not composed of matter and form.

Objection: If someone claims the soul is composed of matter and form, William argues that the form is incorruptible because it has no contrary.

Objection: If someone argues that, as sight is corrupted by visible things, so the intellect is by intelligible things, William answers that sight is so corrupted because it has a bodily organ.

Objection: If someone argues that the intellect is not form at all, William answers that the intellect is in itself something formed, but able to receive all the intelligibles that are external to it.

The human soul cannot be destroyed by the division of its integral parts, because it is necessarily without parts.

If the intellect had parts, it would not understand as a whole and would not understand something instantaneously, but part by part.

The human soul cannot be destroyed by the withdrawl of its cause, since the activities of the first cause continuously flow forth upon the natural world and the soul.

Objection: If someone says that the sensitive soul is also immortal, William has already answered that point.

6. The difference between the senses and the intellective power shows that the latter is immortal.

Because the intellect is not changed, much less harmed by the objects it knows.

Because the more intelligible its objects are, the more the intellect is strengthened.

Because the intellect does not have an end in its activity.

Objection: The activity of the intellect is finite. William distinguishes between particular acts of intellection and intellection without qualification.

Objection: The intellect has an end in the first light. William concedes this, because the intellect has its ultimate rest, on this view, in the source of life itself.

5. Sources and Influences

Though the *De immortalitate animae* is the work of a Christian theologian and even of the bishop of Paris, it is intended to be a philosophical work and consciously eschews any appeal to the authority of Scripture or writings of the saints. William is well aware that he "will not effectively prevail over those erroneous philosophers against whom we are arguing" by employing such authorities.[35] He explicitly mentions his intention to use the authority of Aristotle first of all. But his use of Aristotle or of Aristotelian arguments and authorities is less clear than his announced intention might lead one to suppose. Though one can at times trace a line of argument back to the *De anima* of Aristotle, one is left with the impression that William may well have known Aristotle chiefly through his Arabian followers rather than at first hand.

William states that he is going to rely upon the authority of Aristotle and refers vaguely to the second book of his *De anima*.[36] Later he explicitly acknowledges that he has taken his first two "proper" arguments from "the philosophers, namely, Aristotle and his followers."[37] Aristotle is explicitly mentioned a third time in an objection where the objector appeals to Aristotle's doctrine that motion is the continuous and not the instantaneous transition from potency to act.[38] William calls the objector "mistaken, feeble-minded and an obstacle to himself" for quibbling over words and neglecting the truth.

William mentions Plato twice. He appeals to Plato's statement "in the book on the immortality of the soul" that souls that withdraw from external things into themselves experience their freedom from the region

35. Cf. translation, pp. 24-25.
36. Cf. translation, p. 25.
37. Cf. translation, p. 33. The expression, *Aristoteles et sequaces ejus,* is frequent in William of Auvergne. R. de Vaux mentions that the expression was not invented by William since he borrows it at least once from Gundissalinus's *De immortalitate animae* (ed. Bülow, p. 11). Of course, if the latter is actually the work of William, there is no borrowing of this expression from Gundissalinus. Cf. de Vaux, *Notes et textes sur l'Avicennisme latin* (Paris: J. Vrin, 1934), pp. 30-38, for William's use of "Aristotle and his followers." De Vaux shows that these followers are the Arabian philosophers, especially, Al Farabi, Algazeli and Avicenna.
38. Cf. translation, p. 34. Bülow claims that he is unable to find anywhere in Aristotle where he speaks of every motion as continuous, though he points to *Physics* 262a and 267a where he speaks of continuous motion.

of death. Here he seems to allude to Plato's *Phaedo*.[39] Later he explains that he has taken his first two demonstrative arguments from Aristotle and passed over those of Plato, because the arguments of Plato are not convincing for intelligent people and are common to all kinds of souls, that is, to the souls of plants and animals, as well as to human souls.[40]

Otherwise, William mentions no philosophers by name. He mentions the example of St. Peter in debate with Simon Magus. In doing so, he reveals his familiarity with what we know as the pseudo-Clementine literature.[41] William also mentions the *Dialogues* of Gregory the Great.[42] He appeals to the first case as a justification for his using proofs from grounds that are not "proper." He mentions the writings of Gregory only to dismiss them as not providing suitable philosophical material. No other proper names occur in the work.

There are, however, several passages in which William is clearly dependent upon Aristotelian doctrine. For instance, he says that "nature is the source of motion and rest," which reflects *Physics* II, 1, 192b21 and *De caelo* I, 2, 268b11.[43] So too, William's first root principle drawn from the philosophers would seem to have its ultimate source in Aristotle's *De anima* I, 1, 403a10-11, and another root principle, namely, that "no motion of nature is naturally pointless or in vain" reflects *De caelo* I, 4, 271a33.[44] Similarly, he recognizes the legitimacy of Aristotle's claim that a demonstration must draw its premises from the proper genus, which is based on *Posterior Analytics* I, 7, 75a38-39.[45] Aristotle's *De anima* I, 4, 408b8-25 is at least the remote source of William's doctrine that the intellect does not age and fail as the body grows old.[46] William seems to allude to Aristotle's doctrine that the intellect can become all things (*De anima* III, 4, 429a19-22) when he says that the intellect "is related to all bodily and spiritual forms by its ability to receive them . . . ."[47] William's talk about "perfection" as "the attainment of only those things which are potentially present in what can be perfected" would seem to reflect the Aristotelian doctrine of *entelecheia*,[48] and his claim that the activities of the senses have a mean or a harmony is probably derived from Aristotle's *De anima* II, 11, 424a4-6.[49] But there is no conclusive evidence that William had a direct familiarity with any of Aristotle's works.

---

39. Cf. translation, p. 24.
40. Cf. translation, p. 33 and note 26.
41. Cf. translation, p. 25, and note 10.
42. Cf. translation, p. 24, and note 5.
43. Cf. translation, p. 55.
44. Cf. translation, pp. 27 and 34.
45. Cf. translation, p. 25.
46. Cf. translation, p. 28 and note 17.
47. Cf. translation, p. 48.
48. Cf. translation, p. 35.
49. Cf. translation, p. 40.

From his study of the sources Bülow concludes that "the writing *De immortalitate animae* presents a compilation of Dominicus Gundissalinus, the majority of which rests upon an Arabian source. The author and title of this latter remains for us shrouded in darkness."[50] Gilson calls attention to the fact that the style of the author of the treatise – he is thinking of Gundissalinus – is naturally that of Gundissalinus's own Latin translations of Avicenna, even though he has just noted that William uses the same Avicennian style in his *De anima*.[51] Gilson does, however, make the helpful suggestion that with regard to *De immortalitate animae* the possible influence of Avicenna has not been sufficiently considered and points specifically to *De anima* V, 2 and V, 4.[52]

If the author of *De immortalitate animae* is indeed William of Auvergne, as Allard has argued, then there is solid reason for accepting a major role for Avicenna in terms of the sources for our treatise, since Avicenna certainly is a major influence upon William's *De anima* and upon his metaphysics in the first part of *De trinitate*. Gilson has said that "the Avicennian notion of the soul by itself commits one who holds it to maintain its personal immortality; this in turn implies the recognition of a future life."[53] Though Gilson's statement may well need some qualification, it is certainly true that William, like Avicenna, viewed the human soul as an incorporeal substance. William even quotes with approbation in his *De anima* Avicenna's hypothesis of "the floating man" who, apart from all sensory experience, is able to know himself.[54]

Following Gilson's suggestion that Avicenna's *De anima* V, 2 and V, 4 needed to be more carefully examined as possible sources for the *De immortalitate animae*, I examined these chapters. In *De anima* V, 2, Avicenna develops the Aristotelian statement that the soul does not weaken with the body at the end of youth, thus offering a more proximate source than Aristotle's *De anima* I, 4, 408b18-25.[55] So too, William's contrast between the soul's being occupied and its being injured may well rest upon Avicenna's discussion of the "occupation" of the various powers of the soul in *De anima* IV, 2.[56] William's reference to the estimative power may well also be derived from Avicenna, especially when this is coupled with the localization of this power in the middle compartment of the brain.[57] Avicenna's development of Aristotle's *De anima* III, 4, 429a29-

---

50. Bülow, p. 107.
51. Gilson, "Avicenne en occident au moyen age," p. 101-102, note 12.
52. Ibid.
53. Ibid.
54. Cf. translation, note 16.
55. Cf. translation, pp. 28-29.
56. Cf. translation, p. 29.
57. Cf. G. Klubertanz, *The Discursive Power: Sources and Doctrine of the* Vis Cogitativa *According to St. Thomas Aquinas* (St. Louis: The Modern Schoolman, 1952), pp. 90-91, 95 and 126, and translation, p. 32.

429b4 in *De anima* V, 2, may provide the more proximate source for the idea that forceful objects of the senses prevent the sense from perceiving less forceful objects immediately afterwards and that the case is just the opposite with the intellect.[58] So too, William's talk about intermediate causes between the soul and the first cause and about the continuous outpouring of the activities of the first cause upon the soul and nature could well reflect Avicenna's doctrine of mediating intelligences and of the necessary outpourings of the activities of the first cause.[59] The absence of any reference to bodily resurrection in William's discussion of immortality may also be the result of an Avicennian influence.[60] Thus certain passages in *De immortalitate animae* would seem to have Avicenna as a proximate source, though, on the basis of *De immortalitate animae* alone, he would hardly be considered a major influence upon William's thought.

William says that he is writing against "erroneous philosophers" who have denied the immortality of the soul, but he nowhere identifies his opponents.[61] Though Averroes comes to mind as the most likely opponent of personal immortality, there is no indication that William is arguing against a specifically Averroistic doctrine. Furthermore, it seems unlikely that Averroes was sufficiently known in the West before 1230.[62] R. de Vaux has suggested that William concluded from his reading of Avicenna that the latter had to deny personal immortality.[63] It may well be that William has in mind such conclusions which William clearly drew from Avicennian principles. I mentioned above that Gilson's claim linking the

---

58. Cf. translation, pp. 40-41.

59. Cf. translation, p. 51. That is, this passage seems to reflect elements of Arabian thought that are not compatible with William's mature positions. In this regard, cf. translation, p. 54 and note 80, where there seems to be a correction of an earlier position by the later version of the text.

60. Cf. Alan E. Bernstein, "Esoteric Theology: William of Auvergne on the Fires of Hell and Purgatory," *Speculum* 57 (1982) 509-531.

61. Cf. translation, p. 24.

62. De Vaux also points out that William mentions Averroes only two times and calls him "philosophus nobilissimus." Cf. *De anima* ch. III, pt. 11 (II, 101a) and *De Universo* II, c. 8 (I, 851b). On the other hand, William cites Avicenna about forty times. Cf. de Vaux, "Notes et textes," pp. 21-22. Cf. also his, "La première entrée d'Averroës chez les Latins," *Revue des sciences philosophiques et théologiques* 22 (1933) 235-236, where de Vaux argues from William's rudimentary knowledge of Averroes that the translations of his works were just becoming known in Paris in the early 1230's.

63. Cf. de Vaux, *Notes et textes*, pp. 27-30, where he argues that, without any other principle of individuation save matter, logic demanded that, once human souls are separated from their bodies, they cannot on Avicennian principles remain many. In *De universo* I, 852b-853b, William says, "On the first of the previously mentioned questions you have heard the statement of Aristotle and the statements of Al Farabi and Avicenna and the others who have agreed with Aristotle on this matter. They have all been of one mind on this opinion that all diversity, all plurality derives from corporeal matter. For this reason they agreed that even our souls, when they are separated from their bodies, neither constitute nor have a plurality, but all of them are one substance and one thing, and that they do not discover among them diversity . . . ."

Avicennian view of the soul with personal immortality might well need qualification. In the light of William's inference that Avicenna denied that there was a plurality of human souls once they were separated from their bodies on the grounds that matter is the only cause of plurality, it seems that Avicenna was most likely one of the "erroneous philosophers" against whose doctrine William was arguing, even though William shared with Avicenna the view of the soul as a spiritual substance. Hence, the absence of any explicit appeal in the *De immortalitate animae* to Avicenna's doctrine becomes quite understandable, since the work was aimed directly at what William took to be his position, namely, that there was no personal survival of the human soul.[64]

Bülow has pointed out a number of possible allusions to Ibn Gabirol's *Fons vitae*. For example, he speaks of "the source of life" three times.[65] Bülow also points to a number of expressions that are likely drawn from *Fons vitae*, e.g., the unusual verb, *approximare*, found in *Fons vitae* III, 55, p. 201 and in *De immortalitate*, p. 8, and the expression, *in ultima uilitatis* (*Fons vitae* III, 57, p. 205), which is reflected in *ultimum uilitatis* (*De immortalitate*, p. 17). Similarly, Bülow points to the expression, *vivere ejus in effectu*, from *De immortalitate*, p. 20, as reflecting *Fons vitae* III, 23, p. 132. So too, William's frequent use of *radices* for the root or basic principles of his demonstrations may also reflect the usage of *Fons vitae* III, 38, p. 166 (*radices ipsarum probationum*). Bülow also finds an allusion to *Fons vitae* III, 37, p. 165, in *De immortalitate*, p. 21, though there are, it seems, much better sources for the doctrine of the two faces of the intellective power. Though there is evidence that the author of *De immortalitate animae* was familiar with the *Fons vitae*, it is also clear, as Bülow has pointed out that the author of our work explicitly rejects the characteristic doctrine of Ibn Gabirol, namely, universal hylomorphism.[66]

An investigation of the sources of the *De immortalitate animae* cannot overlook the doctrine of the two faces of the intellective power.[67] Bülow points to parallels in Gundissalinus's *De anima* and in Algazali's

---

64. The metaphysical problem of what individuates souls that are pure forms does not seem to have an adequate philosophical answer in William. In response to the Avicennian claim that matter is the principle of individuation and the consequent lack of a plurality of souls after their separation from the body, William appeals to the fact that "every law and every prophecy" contradicts this and argues that any inequality of reward or punishment would be impossible (*De universo* II, c. 9 [I, 853a]).

65. Cf. translation, pp. 24 and 55. Bülow notes that the same expression is found in Psalm 35:10 as well as many other Biblical passages, but believes that the author, Gundissalinus, as he thought, was alluding to the work he had translated.

66. Cf. translation, p. 47, where William says that the human soul is "pure form and an immaterial substance."

67. Cf. translation, p. 40 and note 40.

Liber philosophiae, but rejects Avicenna's *De anima* as a source.[68] So too, the discussion of ecstasy and rapture, which surely has a source in the Neoplatonic tradition, is perhaps remotely grounded in Augustine's discussion of St. Paul's being rapt to the third heaven.[69]

Finally, there is in *De immortalitate animae* an argument that the soul is without parts because it is acted upon as a whole at once and not part by part.[70] If the intellect were acted upon part by part, William continues, it would understand spoken syllables and words successively as they are heard and not all at once as the intellect grasps their meaning. William also argues that the intellect as a whole understands whenever it understands, not a part first and another part later.[71] The argument bears an interesting resemblance to Plotinus's argument in *Ennead* V,3,1 and to Augustine's argumentation in *De trinitate* X,iii,5-iv,6.[72]

This examination of the sources of the *De immortalitate animae* confirms Bülow's judgment that the work is a compilation. It is most likely based upon sources in the Christian tradition as well as upon Aristotelian philosophy as mediated by Avicenna, Algazali and Ibn Gabirol. But in a sense it is unfair to regard it as no more than a compilation, for it is a creative response to an intellectual challenge, even if it draws upon the ideas of others. The work reveals an author in the Christian tradition faced with philosophical arguments that denied the immortality of the soul; it also reveals one who clearly saw that philosophical arguments had to be met with philosophical arguments and who judiciously drew upon the wealth of new material suddenly available to the West to formulate an answer within an Avicennian framework to the group of erring philosphers that clearly included Avicenna himself.

It is less easy to document the influence of the work. Gilson says of the arguments it contains that they "will be endlessly reproduced: independence of the intellect from the body, immateriality of the soul as form, natural desire, union of the soul with the Source of Life, etc."[73] It is true that such arguments occur again and again in medieval authors, but it is impossible to credit this to William's influence, for the next generation of philosophers and theologians had a much better acquaintance with the sources and they also incorporated their discussion of the immortality of the soul into various questions in their *Summae* or into commentaries on

---

68. Cf. note 40 and Bülow, p. 127, note 1. Bülow sees here an allusion to Ibn Gabirol's *Fons vitae* III, 37, p. 165, where he speaks of the soul as between the substance of the intellect and sense so that it turns to one and the other, but there are clearer antecedents in Gundissalinus's *De anima* and in Algazali's *Liber philosophiae*, as Bülow has shown.

69. Cf. Augustine, *De Genesi ad litteram* XII: *BA* 49, 328-456.

70. Cf. translation, pp. 49-50.

71. Cf. translation, p. 50.

72. Cf. note 68.

73. E. Gilson, *History of Christian Philosophy in the Middle Ages* (New York: Random House, 1955), p. 653, note 4.

the *De anima* of Aristotle rather than in separate treatises on immortality. Nonetheless, despite William's less direct contact with the sources, he did isolate the main lines of argumentation that, as Gilson said, would be endlessly reproduced.

6. The Text Translated and Some Conventions

The translation follows the text attributed by Bülow to Dominicus Gundissalinus; it is based upon the following manuscripts: P: Parisinus bibliotecae nationalis lat. 16613, s. xiii; M: Parisinus bibliotecae nationalis lat. 14988, s. xiii; N: Parisinus bibliotecae nationalis lat. 14887, s. xiv; and C: Carnotensis bibliotecae publicae 377, s. xiv. To refer to the text Bülow attributed to Gundissalinus, I use: g, and to refer to the text he attributed to William, I use: w. I have added to g in italics significant material from w. The text of w is based upon only one manuscript, B: Bruxellensis bibl. reg. 21856, and three editions: n: ed. Nurenburgae, 1496; v: ed. Venetae, 1591, and a: ed. Aureliana. I have used angle brackets to indicate significant material present in g, but not found in w. The numbers in square brackets refer to the pages of Bülow's edition.

The Immortality of the Soul

The Immortality of the Soul

[1] You ought to know from other sources that human errors are taken care of in four *or five* ways. First, by sensation, through experience. Second, by punishment, through the law *that penalizes and draws one back from errors*. Third, by philosophy, *that is*, through *valid* proof. Fourth, *by authority that is worthy of belief and is handed on by an authority or by someone accepted as an authority. Fifthly, in a still more lofty way, that is*, in a divine way, namely, through prophecy or revelation *or through a teaching handed on immediately by God. The divine goodness has bestowed upon us these five ways, like five divine remedies or salves clearing the eyes, to heal blindness regarding errors and spiritual things.*

Here one can see how harmful and destructive the divine goodness considers an error *of faith and morals* and especially that *error* which concerns the natural mortality *of rational souls*. For *that error* destroys the foundation of morality and of all religion. For souls that lack a belief in their immortality, since they have no hope of another life and, hence, no assurance that they will attain true happiness, what remains but to surrender to all the vices? What will they consider morality to be but madness? For when they see that they are cheated of present *delights* and expect no others, they can in no way be convinced that a belief in moral goodness is anything else than a delusion of the ignorant [2] and that the profession of praiseworthy morals is the raving of those who have been deceived. From these beliefs there follow an intolerable disturbance of human affairs, a complete confusion of life *and conduct*, and the worst of all evils, namely, the *most audacious* dishonoring of the Creator.[1]

Rightly, then, has the divine mercy applied so many remedies to so harmful an error. Thus the law by its penalties heals those who are contemptuous, and philosophy by its proofs heals those who lack knowledge, and prophecy heals through revelation those willing to respect the

---

1. William says in *De anima* ch. V, pt. 22 (II, 147a), at the beginning of his treatise on the immortality of the soul, "You have already heard from me how useful this knowledge of immortality is for the knowledge of God and of morals and for the settling and ordering of the whole of human life. This is apparent from the fact that souls who are unaware of their immortality believe nothing at all and they think that they should care nothing concerning the goodness of conduct, nothing concerning the perfections of the virtues, and nothing at all concerning the glory of future happiness, and that is the way they act." It would seem that William is alluding to the beginning of *De immortalitate animae* and that he regards it as his own work. References to William's works other than *The Trinity* and *The Immortality of the Soul* will be to the part, chapter, volume and page of the Orléans-Paris edition: *Guilelmi Alverni Episcopi Parisiensis Opera Omnia*, 2 vols., ed. F. Hotot, and *Supplementum*, ed. Blaise Le Feron (Orléans-Paris, 1674; reprinted Frankfurt am Main, 1963).

divine *Scripture*. The senses also heal those who desire to experience *the immortality of souls*, not only by accepting the testimony of those who rise and return from the other life, but also *by accepting the testimony* of their own souls, if they are willing to withdraw themselves from the body and from other *things* and gather themselves to themselves. For these *souls returning in this way from external things to themselves, as Plato says in the book on the immortality of the soul,*[2] without any doubt perceive that they are apart from the region of death, and they recognize their continuity *and union* with the source of life and that there is nothing standing between them and the source of life that might impede and turn aside the outpouring of life upon them.[3] But this experience is impossible for souls *that are* poured out upon and scattered *over the senses and* sensible things and are imprisoned in their own bodies.

In the present work we will try to teach how philosophy meets this error with the proofs *of authorities and with arguments.*[4] We have not undertaken the task of setting forth here the authorities of the New and Old Testaments and of the early saints and the experiences recorded in the *Dialogues* of blessed Pope Gregory and in other writings like them, for they can easily be discovered by others.[5] Through such means, moreover, we will not effectively prevail over those erroneous philosophers

---

2. The reference to Plato may be to *Phaedo* 64E-65C and 67C, where he speaks of the soul of the philosopher withdrawing from the body and gathering itself within itself.

3. William alludes to Ibn Gabirol's work, *The Source of Life* (*Fons vitae*), which Dominicus Gundissalinus had translated into Latin. References to *The Source of Life* will be by book, section, and page of the edition by Clemens Baeumker, *Avencebrolis (Ibn Gabirol) Fons vitae ex arabico in latinam translatus ab Ioanne Hispano et Dominico Gundissalino* in *Beiträge zur Geschichte der Philosophie des Mittelalters* I (Münster: Aschendorff, 1892). In his *The Trinity* (*De trinitate*) XII, 115, William refers to Ibn Gabirol, or Avicebron, as the most noble of all philosophers. William believed him to be a Christian. References to William's *The Trinity* will be by chapter and page in the English translation: William of Auvergne, *The Trinity, or The First Principle* translated from the Latin by Roland J. Teske, S.J. and F. C. Wade, S.J. (Milwaukee: Marquette University Press, 1989). The critical edition of the Latin is edited by Bruno Switalski, *William of Auvergne: De trinitate: An Edition of the Latin Text with an Introduction* (Toronto: Pontifical Institute of Mediaeval Studies, 1976).

4. William intends this work to be philosophical and realizes that, in arguing against philosophers, he must use philosophical authorities and arguments, not the authorities of Scripture or of the Fathers which would be ineffective against his present opponents. He does not reject all use of authorities, but only those which are not philosophical. Thus, he appeals to the authority of Aristotle, while rejecting that of the Old and New Testaments and of writings like that of Gregory the Great.

5. In his *Dialogues*, especially Book Four, which deals with death and the afterlife, Gregory the Great produces many stories involving persons who returned from the dead and appeared to those still living. For the Latin cf. *PL* LXXVII, 149-430; for a modern edition with ample annotation, cf. *SC* 251, 260 and 265. In *De anima* ch. VI, pt. 30 (II, 189b-190b), William sets forth testimonies from pagan literature and from the Old and New Testaments to immortality and resurrection. For example, he alludes to Aeneas's descent to the underworld to see the soul of his father, to the raising of Lazarus, to a restoration to life of a Roman emperor by the prayers of a holy pontiff, and other reports of resurrections. In pt. 31 (II, 190b-191b), he amasses testimony from the saints and prophets.

whom we are here arguing. There are, then, authorities for these matters and, first of all, the authority of Aristotle who speaks of this in the second book of *On the Soul.*[6]

Return to the notes[7] for authorities that you have studied. You already know from the teaching of logic that a syllogism amounts to a demonstration only when it is drawn from its proper grounds.[8] For when transcendental and extraneous materials are brought to bear upon a conclusion whose certitude we are seeking—I mean: brought to bear in a syllogistic structure and order, they do not produce demonstrative knowledge for us. [3] Still ignorance and failure and the eagerness for somehow knowing the truth force us to be satisfied with such syllogisms. For this reason we were not the first to set forth the justice of the Creator and the future judgment as a root principle[9] in proof of the immortality of the soul, but others did so before us, namely, the apostle Peter arguing against Simon Magus in the *Itinerarium* of Clement, Pope and Martyr.[10]

For if the human soul would not live after this life, it would be vain and pointless to serve God here. After all, in this life the worship of God and religion involves much torment and affliction for the soul, and after this life there would be no reward for it, since there would not even be life for the human soul after this life. Accordingly, it would be more advantageous for the human soul utterly to deny God and *give itself over* to every vanity and pleasure than to live a holy and just life and to worship the Creator with due honor and devotion.[11] If God has care for those who

---

6. William appeals to Aristotle's *De anima*, Book Two, though he does not derive the "root principles" for the arguments he presents from Book Two as much as from Books One and Three.

7. The Latin *"quaternum"* seems to refer to a booklet in which the student kept notes on a particular subject, here logic. William presupposes that his readers have studied logic.

8. Aristotle, *Posterior Analytics* I, 7, 75a38-39. Aristotle says that "we cannot in demonstrating pass from one genus to another. We cannot, for instance, prove geometrical truths by arithmetic." As we shall see, William's first set of arguments are based upon various divine attributes; the demonstrative proofs have to be based upon the nature and activities of the soul.

9. William uses *"radix"* which is literally root, but has the transferred meaning of principle or axiom. The *radices* that William uses are the major premises in various arguments for the soul's immortality. Ibn Gabirol refers to "the root principles of proofs" in *Fons vitae* III, 38, p. 166.

10. The reference is to the Pseudo-Clementine writings in which there is recorded a debate between St. Peter and Simon Magus. Cf. the old edition of *The Catholic Encyclopedia* on "Clementines," IV, pp. 39-44 (New York: Robert Appleton, 1907-1912). Cf. pp. 122-124, in *Die Pseudoklementinen* II. *Rekognitionen in Rufins Übersetzung*, ed. by Bernhard Rehm (Berlin: Akademie Verlag, 1965).

11. In his *De anima* ch. VI, pt. 22 (II, 176b), William says that he is going "to establish the immortality of the soul by the paths of proofs concerning God in the manner of wisdom" *(per vias probationum sapientialium ac divinalium)*. He explains, "I said that the proofs should be said to concern God, because God himself the most high is the strongest and most irrefragable root of them all." He then sets forth proofs from his goodness (pt. 22), his providence (pt. 23), his goodness again (pt. 25), his justice (pt. 26), his generosity (pt. 28), and his glory (pt. 29).

worship and venerate him, where *then* is his power? For *those who do not worship him* are not for that reason worse off in this life, and *those who do worship him* are not better off in another life, since there will not be another *life* after this one *according to the error that claims that the human soul will die with the body.* If, however, he does not have such care, where *then* is his wisdom or goodness? He seems either not to be aware of or not to love those who love and venerate him. The one alternative destroys his wisdom; the other his goodness. This, then, is the first root principle for the matter at hand by which we have tried to show that the human soul has a life after this life.

Another root principle for us is the very justice of God, given which it is necessary that there be a future judgment. In this life neither the bad nor the good receive what they deserve, for the bad fare well here and the good fare poorly. Where, then, is the justice of God when each of them, *namely, the good and the bad,* receive in this life what is contrary to their merits, if after this life there will not be a *general* judgment, which, of course, will not be if there is not a life after this life?

[4] We use a third root principle for this same point, *namely, to show that there is another life.* It is this, *namely,* that all *perfect* justice proceeds to judgment, and neither ignorance of merits, nor some difficulty or impossibility of repayment holds back such *justice.* But it is impossible that the divine justice be held back or impeded by any of these. Hence, it is necessary that it proceed to *perfect* judgment *at some time,* and it does not do so in this life, *as we admit on the basis of the examples we have mentioned.* Hence, it will do so after this life.[12]

We often use this fourth root principle *to show the same thing,* namely, that the most wise and good God has provided something better for his elect than this life holds, since under the guidance of *divine* wisdom *the elect* disdain whatever this life holds and this life itself, *as a result of the advice of God himself, as is obvious to those who read the Gospels and Letters and the whole Old and New Testaments, where it treats of the contempt of worldly things.* Hence, the wise especially would be found to be in error and deceived, though wisdom itself is their guide, when they

---

12. In *De anima* ch. VI, pt. 26 (II, 185a-b), William says, "It is clear from these considerations that such justice, if it is living and true, must proceed to judgment, and that it is held back or prevented from this neither by ignorance, nor by impossibility, nor by difficulty in doing what is just. Since, then, the justice of the Creator is always living and true, it must proceed to judgment and reward each according to his merits, namely, the good with good things for their pleasing service and the bad with bad things for their evil deeds. For with God there is no place for an ignorance of deserving people or their merits. . . . Since, then, in this present life the justice of God does not exercise judgment to the full extent, since very many bad people receive only good things here and, likewise, very many good people suffer only evil things here, it is necessary that there be in the next life a reward or repayment of whatever is owed through this justice."

disdain and cast aside their entire good. Only the evil would live here wisely and act prudently, since they alone seek in this life their own good.[13] There remains, then, that God will provide something better for his elect and those who worship him than this life holds, and this will not take place in this life. For there is nothing better in this life than what this life holds; therefore, it will take place in another life, and there is *another* life besides this one at least for the souls of the good. Hence, there will be another life also for the souls of the bad. For if God has prepared nothing worse for the souls of the bad than what this life holds, then the bad not only go unpunished, but they are bad *even to their own advantage, because in this life they use many temporal goods and are freed from many temporal evils, as their wickedness provides for them. Hence, if there is not another life, it is better for the bad in terms of their own wickedness. How, in the judgment of any rational mind*, will the divine righteousness tolerate this?

Now we will attempt to establish the soul's immortality from its proper grounds.[14]

[5] First, then, we will set in order the root principles we have received from the philosophers, of which this is the first.

If the activity of a substance does not depend on the body, its essence does not depend upon the body.[15] For the essence of any substance must be more free from the body than the activity. Since, then, the activity of the human soul, the activity < of that which is most subtle and noble in the human soul, > namely, that by which we surpass the brute animals, does not depend upon the body, as is the case with the activity of the intellect, < it is clear that > its essence does not depend upon it either. Hence, it is naturally separable from the body and has life apart from the body.

---

13. In *De anima* ch. VI, pt. 24 (II, 182a) William says, "Moreover, either the goodness of the Creator has provided some good things for his beloved and elect other than temporal and present ones, and I mean those which are had in the present life, or he has not. If he has not provided such goods, they do not have either freedom from present miseries or happiness and well-being, since it is not possible for them to attain either in the present life. For well-being is not possible amid miseries, nor can happiness exist amid miseries, as you have already heard. Since they are the ones who are most afflicted with sorrows here, their condition and state is necessarily worse than is that of the bad. Hence, they are rendered vain in accord with the words that say: 'Vain is he who serves God, and fruitless are their labors' (Ml 3:14). They are, then, wretchedly deceived, and they act most foolishly, while believing wisdom and having wisdom as their guide. But the bad alone live wisely, who love, seek and obtain only present and temporal goods."

14. That is, up to this point, William's arguments are based on attributes of God; now he will begin to present arguments that are based on the nature of the soul.

15. William's first root principle ultimately derives from Aristotle; cf. *De anima* I, 1, 403a10-11: "If there is any way of acting or being acted upon proper to the soul, soul will be capable of separate existence."

Moreover, in accord with the same argument, if the activity of a power is not impeded by the body, its being or essence does not depend upon the body. But it is obvious that the intellective power is of this sort, because the more it becomes involved with <and immersed in> the body, the more its intellectual knowing will be obscure, dull, slow and mixed with errors. But the more it separates and withdraws itself from the body, the more it will be sharp, clear, quick and free from errors. We understand here spiritual, not bodily separation, and we understand in a similar way its drawing near, which is its solicitude for and love of the body and of what belongs to the body. It is clear that, while the opposite things free and clarify it, such solicitude and love immerse and obscure the intellect, and these things are like the presence of the body and its attractiveness for the intellect. The essence, then, of the intellect does not depend upon the body, since its *proper* activity is impeded by it and through it.[16]

Moreover, if the essence of the intellect depends upon the body, the strengthening of the former should follow the strengthening of the latter and the weakening of former should follow the weakening of the latter. But we see the whole matter is just the opposite. For the weakening [6] of the body occurs in old age, and the vigor of the intellective power is then greatest and the intellect in every way is strongest. From this it is clearly obvious that the intellective power is rejuvenated in old age.[17]

---

16. With Avicenna, William viewed man as the soul. William even goes so far as to maintain that the soul is not a part of man, but the man. The body is an instrument. William cites with approval Avicenna's "floating man" hypothesis. "These matters being as they are, I shall return to where I was, and I am aiming at an explanation of the spirituality of the human soul. I will set forth for you the explanation that Avicenna produces for this point. He says, then, that, if we placed a man in the air who has his face covered and is not using any sense and who has not used any sense, there is no doubt but that it is possible for this man to think and understand. Hence, he will know that he thinks or understands, and he will know that this is what he is. If he asks himself whether he has a body, he will doubtless say that he does not have a body, and in the same way he will deny of himself each and every part of the human body. He will deny that he has a head, likewise that he has feet and hands, and so on for the rest. He will admit that he has being and he will deny, Avicenna says, that he has a body. For him the being which he admits concerning himself will not be that which he denies of himself. Since he will deny of himself being a body, while he admits of himself his own being which he either has or perceives that he has, it is necessary that the soul have being which is not the body's, and for this reason it is necessary that it not be the body" (*De anima* ch. 2, pt. 13 [II, 82b-83a]). Cf. Avicenna, *De anima* I, 1, pp. 36-37. References to Avicenna's *De anima* are to the part, chapter and pages in *Avicenna Latinus: Liber de anima seu Sextus de naturalibus*, ed. by S. van Reit; introduction by G. Verbeke (Louvain: Editions orientalistes; Leiden: E. J. Brill, 1968).

17. In his *De anima* V, 2, p. 99, Avicenna says, "Likewise, the powers of all the parts of the body are weakened at the end of youth, which occurs at about forty years. But this power that apprehends intelligibles frequently does not attain its strength until after this age. Hence, if it were one of the bodily powers, it ought at that time to be weakened." Ultimately, the idea goes back to Aristotle's *De anima* I, 4, 408b18-25.

Moreover, everything mortal is gradually weakened by its duration and fails until it comes to the final failure that is death. But the intellective power makes progress through its duration and grows stronger so that, the longer it lasts and older it is, the stronger it is in every way. The intellective power, then, is immortal, and it is clear that it not only cannot age or approach failure by reason of its duration, but that from its duration it grows young and is further removed from failure and death. Here the difference between an animal power and the intellective power also becomes obvious. For an animal power, as dependent upon the body, follows its dispositions. When the body is strengthened, it grows strong; when the body is vigorous, it is vigorous, and when the body is weakened, it is weakened. When the body fails, it fails, insofar as it is an animal power, and the animal activities cease entirely. But the intellective power behaves in just the opposite way with respect to the body.[18]

If someone objects that the intellective power is impeded and weakened when the body is impeded and weakened, as in those who are ill, for example, in those who are delirious, out of their minds, melancholy and mentally alienated in some other manner, we answer that to impede or injure is not the same as to occupy.[19] For we do not say that exterior sight or hearing injures or impedes the intellect, but that it truly occupies the human mind so that it is not free at that time for intellective activity, because [7] it is drawn through sight or *through* hearing to particular external things. It is that way too with the emotions in those under their influence. These sorts of emotions are like persistent dreams that recur on account of impressions that cannot be removed or readily be removed. As dreams, then, hold the mind or the soul occupied with and bound by phantasms, so do these alienated states. They do not harm the essence of the intellective power, but impede its activity by occupying it. This is obvious, because, when the animal power has been set free and cleansed completely from this sort of impression, the intellective power returns to its proper activities as though it had suffered no harm in its essence. And amid these disturbances and alienations, as if it were freed and released

---

18. In *De anima* ch. VII, pt. 5 (II, 162b), William uses much the same argument, "But if the soul grows old and is weakened by its drawing near to death, then it is necessary that, the older it gets, that is, the longer the time it lives, the weaker it will become, and it will do so naturally or in accord with its nature. But it is clear that just the opposite is the case, since its noble and higher powers are stronger, more agile and freer in old age than in youth or adolescence." The following part (II, 163a-b) continues the same argument, "It has already been explained to you . . . that the human soul naturally becomes youthful as the body grows old. Just as growing old is to approach death by becoming weaker, so it is necessary that by becoming youthful through growing strong it is separated from death."

19. In his *De anima* IV, 2, pp. 13-16, Avicenna has a long discussion of how various powers of the soul can be occupied so that the soul is prevented from attending to other things.

from the body, it breaks forth into divine prophecies and revelations.[20] But it is certain that prophecy and revelation are the strongest and most noble activities of the intellective power while it is in the body, and it is very much strengthened for these by the greatest bodily impediments and injuries. This is the reason why prophetic illumination or revelation hardly ever occurs except with a great weakening of the body, as occurs in ecstasy. And it is for this reason that common usage calls ecstasy rapture.[21] From these facts it is clear that the most noble and strongest activity of the intellective power, which is prophecy or revelation, is most vigorous when the body is weakest, as is obvious in ecstasy or rapture. But this *is* its greatest separation from the body while it is in the body. In the complete separation from the body, then, which is death, it is in full vigor.

Moreover, the proper activity of the intellective power is totally absorbed in its complete union with the body, which is its complete solicitude and complete love for it. [8] On the contrary, then, in its complete separation from the body, its activity will be strengthened and invigorated. This separation occurs in death or, rather, is death itself. But it is impossible that the activity of a power be strengthened along with an injuring of its essence. Hence, the essence of the intellective power is in no way injured as a result of the death of the body. Indications of this,

----

20. In *De anima* ch. VI, pt. 31 (II, 191a), William says that "the prophetic splendor is a vision far more lofty and noble than philosophical knowledge and sciences. It is the light, or illumination, of divine radiance; indeed, it is the revelation of hidden or concealed matters which cannot be seen or known by the light of the human intellect or sense. Hence, it is not without good reason called revelation as the unveiling or uncovering of what is reported. It is called vision by antonomasia, or the excellence of seeing. For this reason one who is now called a prophet was in antiquity called a seer, because with regard to prophetic matters, namely, those which were seen only by the prophetic splendor, only prophets saw and still see. The rest of men are not without good reason regarded as not seeing or as blind in comparison."

21. William frequently appeals to the states of rapture and ecstasy as proofs of the soul's independence of the body. In *De anima* ch. VI, pt. 32 (II, 191b-192a) William discusses ecstasy. He mentions that he has not elsewhere discussed the topic, that is, he has not said anything about its nature. He does clearly appeal to these phenomena in the present work. William adds, moreover, that no one else whose writings have come down to him has dealt with these states. He defines ecstasy as "the departure of the mind, in accord with the meaning of the word, and the proper raising of the human mind above itself as if upon a height from which it sees itself and its own and other things as if below itself . . . ." In the following chapter he speaks of rapture and notes that love (*amor*) is a rapture and a disease by which the lover is so caught up that he can hardly think of anything but the woman he loves (cf. II, 192a). While such rapture is a disease, the rapture in question here is "the most noble love (reading *dilectio* for *directio*) and illumination of the mind . . . through it noble and lofty things snatch human souls from themselves and from other things, transferring or bringing to themselves all the concern of these souls so that at that time they totally occupy the human souls and hold them in dependence upon themselves." Despite his disclaimer regarding any source for this doctrine, apart from Scripture, William's position is, I suspect, influenced by Augustine's treatment of St. Paul's being rapt to the third heaven in *De Genesi ad litteram* XII. For the Scripture and Augustinian background, cf. Joseph Maréchal, "La notion d'extase, d'après l'enseignement traditionel des mystiques et des théologiens," *Nouvelle revue théologique* 64 (1937) 986-998.

however, are clear in rapture or ecstasy or dreams and illnesses which produce alienated states, as we said, and in proximity to death when we have no doubt that prophecies and visions and predictions of the future generally occur.[22] But it is a mark of those who philosophize correctly[23] and who seek to investigate the truth not only to set forth foundations and root principles, but also to add indications and signs.

There is another root principle found among the philosophers, namely, that every substance, whose form is not corruptible, is incorruptible. And every intelligent substance is of this sort, because only *substances in which there are* material forms are corruptible. But no intelligent substance has any of the material forms as its own, that is, as natural and essential. The reason is that such a substance receives the likenesses of all forms, just as the eye has no color in that part of itself where it receives the likenesses of all colors, and taste has no flavor where it receives the likenesses of all flavors.[24] Otherwise, neither the one nor the other would receive the likenesses of the things it senses. It would neither be affected by them, since something white cannot be whitened by white, nor would it be able to receive its likeness in any way. [9] For if it would receive it, there would be found two whitenesses on the same surface, since an impression of whiteness upon what is white could only be whiteness. Since, then, only a material form is corruptible and an intelligent substance cannot have that kind of form as natural or essential, it is

---

22. In *De anima* ch. VI, pt. 5 (II, 161a), William says, "And it is known from experience that the intellective power is strengthened to such an extent by the gravest illnesses of the body that many souls foretell and prophesy about the deaths of their own bodies and at times of others. But they were not capable of this in the health and strength of their bodies."

23. William uses the participle *philosophantes*: those who philosophize. For the use of this term, cf. E. Gilson, "Les philosophantes," *AHDLMA* 19 (1952) 135-140, and P. Michaud-Quantin and M. Lemoine, "Pour le dossier des 'philosophantes'," *AHDLMA* 35 (1968) 17-22. The authors of the latter article note that William of Auvergne showed a predilection for the word and used it no less than thirteen times. They argue that "the bishop of Paris did not look upon them with a favorable eye: neither their doctrines nor their life is commendable" (pp. 19-20). They claim that, when William makes appeal to their testimony, he has to rehabilitate them with the adverbs: "truly and correctly." Cf. *The Trinity*, p. 5, n. 17, where I argue for a more positive sense of "philosophizing" in William. In *The Trinity*, p. 173, William says that the image and likeness of God is brought to its ultimate actuality in the human soul by philosophizing (*philosophando*). There he describes that activity as "doing battle against errors and the darkness of falsity and depravity and against the wickedness of its loves . . . pursuing with a chaste and other-worldy desire and love the light of truth by the light of the true and salutary faith and . . . pursuing the sweetness of goodness by the trace of its scent which is hope." One text from *The Trinity* to which Michaud-Quantin and Lemoine appeal to show that William used *philosophantes* to refer to Neoplatonists could in fact refer to Christians who were influenced by the Neoplatonist doctrine of the preexistence of the soul. In any case William is not there objecting to their doctrine, but citing their position in support of his own. Cf. *The Trinity*, p. 103.

24. Cf. Aristotle, *De anima* III, 4, 419 a 20-21.

clear that an intelligent substance is incorruptible, since its essential form is incorruptible.

They regard this point as certain and proved, because it is most certain that all generation and corruption and all opposition of contraries is found to be in matter and concerning matter. For in immaterial things there is no contrariety and, hence, no opposition, *and* for this reason neither generation nor corruption, since generation and corruption arise from the opposition of contraries that everywhere act upon and are acted upon by one another. For these sorts of actions and passions all take place by contact, and it is necessary that contact take place only in material things and only in bodies.

But if someone asks whether the animal or brute soul is also an immaterial form, one should answer that there are two kinds of material forms. The one totally relies upon and rests in its matter and does not rule it or support it in any way, but is supported by it. This is a bodily form in the proper sense. The other is such that its matter rather relies on it and is supported and ruled by it. The activity of this form, nonetheless, occurs only in its matter and through it. Thus it is apparent that its essence <depends upon its matter, since every one of its activities depends upon it [10] and since its essence> would be idle and useless outside of its matter. The brute and vegetative soul is a material form in this way, that is, dependent upon its matter both as regards its being and as regards its activity. And it is destructible along with the destruction of its matter, just as a fluid kept in a bottle is destroyed with the destruction of the bottle, and fire in wood, although these likenesses are very unlike that for the sake of which they are introduced.

Also this sort of soul is not receptive of all material forms, because it is not receptive of universal forms and perhaps only of sensible forms in the proper sense. For the estimative power, which is certainly found in this sort of soul, perhaps receives only a sensible form in the proper sense. We have said, "in the proper sense," because nothing seems to be a proper matter of estimation for brute animals except what is sensibly harmful or helpful, and the estimative power in brutes is chiefly concerned with these two factors.[25]

---

25. For the history of the estimative power, cf. G. Klubertanz, *The Discursive Power: Sources and Doctrina of the* Vis Cogitativa *according to St. Thomas Aquinas* (St. Louis: The Modern Schoolman, 1952). According to Klubertanz, Al-Farabi (870-950) was the first to single out and name the estimative sense. Avicenna developed and made the doctrine of the internal senses more precise. Cf. Klubertanz, pp. 90-91 and 95 for texts on the estimative power in Avicenna. Algazel followed the teaching of Avicenna (Klubertanz, p. 107). Speaking of the *De immortalitate animae*, Klubertanz follows Gilson and says that the work "is more closely dependent upon Avicenna and Algazel" than Gundissalinus's *De divisione philosophiae* (p. 126).

But how do they establish that in immaterial things there is not an immaterial corruption? After all, there are found in them immaterial emotions and pains, such as, anger, envy, hatred, embarassment, *and others*, all of which are not only emotions and pains, but even the worst of torments. But if there are found in them pains and torments, how will there not also be found there failure and death? How will there be pain and torment without injury? But if there is injury there, it will be possible to come to failure, since the more a cause makes one feel pain, the more it injures. Because, then, every power that can be injured seems limited with regard to suffering, however much the cause of pain happens to be increased, it will be possible to come to the extremity of injury. But this is its failure and death.

On this point we say that pain is spoken of equivocally. A person is said to suffer pain in one way when he is wounded, in another way when he has suffered a loss. [11] The unity between a lover and the beloved is of a far different sort from that among the parts of a continuum. But if unity or connection is equivocal, division will also be equivocal. For whenever one of two contraries is said to be equivocal, the other must also be said to be. In a like manner, injury is spoken of equivocally in these two cases; the one is essential, and the other is not. For by the one injury one is injured in his essence; by the other he is not. Rather he is injured, as we customarily say, in an external possession. And thus as the injury or destruction of the thing does not touch the essence of its owner, so the injury of this sort is not essential. And hence it does not bring about essential failure or injury.

In what follows we will bring you to see that no affection or emotion can of itself bring about an essential failure of this sort. We say this, because nothing in the animal soul prevents an emotion of this sort from becoming so violent that the death of the body results from it and, as a result, the failure of the brute soul. This would likewise happen with regard to the human soul, if its essence depended upon the essence of its body. Now, then, let this point be settled here to this degree until we come to the other things we mentioned.

We have taken almost all of these arguments from the philosophers, namely, from Aristotle and his followers. We pass over, however, the basic arguments and proofs of Plato, because for those with intelligence they do not produce conviction about the immortality of our souls and they are common to all species of souls so that they are also applicable to the brute and *to the* vegetative soul.[26] It is clear that the exis-

---

26. Bülow admits that the criticism is applicable to the arguments in the *Phaedrus* 245e-246a, but not to those in the *Phaedo* 64a-69a, 78b, 107c or those in *Republic* X. But the argument in the *Phaedo* 105b would seem to hold for all souls. There Socrates argues that the soul always brings with it life to whatever it comes and will never admit its opposite.

tence of these souls after the body and apart from the body is pointless and utterly useless. But everything pointless and useless is sought not only without benefit, but [12] also at an expense. For it is sought at the expense and loss of the time in which we should seek useful things.

Let us go back and say that no motion of nature is naturally pointless or in vain and that nothing that is naturally moved is kept by a natural impossibility from the end toward which it is moved.[27] Otherwise, it would be moved toward it pointlessly and in vain. Let us also say that some motions are bodily and that others are spiritual and that fear is spiritual flight and hope is spiritual pursuit. The movements of the heart, namely, contraction and expansion, bear witness to these points, as well as the sensible motions of the body, which are bodily flight and bodily pursuit.[28]

Someone might want to say that all motion is bodily, because motion is the continuous and non-instantaneous transition from potency to act, as Aristotle says, and this definition fits only bodily motion.[29] Such a person is mistaken, feeble-minded and an obstacle to himself as long as he neglects the truth of things and gets involved in a quarrelsome dispute over words. Here we mean by motion only the disposition which by itself is the way of attaining something else, and this account fits all the things

27. William states two root principles: (1) that "no motion of nature is naturally pointless or in vain" and that "nothing that is moved naturally is kept by a natural impossibility from the natural end toward which it is moved." Here he states the second principle negatively, but on the following page he puts it positively: "it is naturally possible to attain everything that is naturally desired." William clearly rests his case upon the Aristotelian principle that God and nature do nothing in vain (*De caelo* I, 4, 271a33). However, his claim that what is naturally desired must be naturally attainable would seem implicitly to deny the supernatural character of perfect human happiness. It is interesting to note that in his *Expositio super librum Boethii de trinitate*, qu. 6, a. 4 (ed. B. Decker [Leiden: Brill, 1955]), St. Thomas says that "everything directed by nature to an end has been previously endowed with principles by which it is able to arrive at that end and by which it also tends toward that end; for the principles of natural motions are within a thing. Now the end of man to which he is directed by nature is to know the immaterial substances, as both the saints and the philosophers teach. So man is naturally endowed with principles of that knowledge" (cf. *Thomas Aquinas: The division and methods of the sciences*, tr. by Armand Maurer [Toronto: Pontifical Institute of Mediaeval Studies, 1953], p. 89). This quotation from Aquinas, however, is from the fifth objection, which might well have been drawn from William's teaching. Cf. Henri de Lubac, *The Mystery of the Supernatural* (New York: Herder and Herder, 1965), p. 150.

28. In *De anima* ch. VII, pt. 13 (II, 168a-170a), William argues for the immortality of the soul from the natural inclination that it has for God. There he says, "You already know that fear is spiritual flight and hope is spiritual pursuit, and the ends of these two motions are escape or evasion, and attainment or acquisition. For one fleeing insofar as he is fleeing aims at evasion or escape. Hence, when that has been acquired, the motion of flight naturally ceases. Likewise, it is clear to you that everyone who is pursuing something aims at the acquisition of it, and for that reason, when it has been attained or acquired, he ceases pursuing the same thing."

29. Bülow notes that Aristotle speaks of motion as *kinêsis sunexês* in *Physics* 262a and 267a, but does not say that all motion is continuous or that motion is not instantaneous; cf. Bülow, p. 120.

that we mentioned. For fear is by itself the way of attaining evasion, and desire is by itself the way of attaining what is desired. Similarly, flight, whether spiritual or bodily, is by itself the way of attaining escape or evasion, and pursuit is the way of attaining possession. And since spiritual things are acquired, just as bodily ones are, it is likewise necessary that there be, for those who acquire them, ways of attaining them in a fitting manner. These ways cease when they have been attained, just as in the attainment of bodily things.

[13] Let us go back to where we were[30] and say that every natural flight aims at a naturally possible evasion, and every pursuit likewise aims at something naturally possible, and that it is possible naturally to attain everything that is naturally desired. Otherwise nature would have taught this sort of desire in vain, because it would be pointless and mistaken, since it would be toward something not an end, even toward something that could not be an end. And thus nature would be in error in the things that it does of itself and does naturally, because every motion and every tending toward something that is not an end is an error.

After having set forth these two root principles, let us consider the proper desires of the human soul insofar as it is human, that is, insofar as it has a noble *being* in which it surpasses the brute soul. We see that it has a desire for true and integral happiness and a flight from true misery, that is, fear and hatred of it. But see that you do not think of the motions of the animal soul and of souls which have already become coarsened by a stupidity that is unnatural and that arises from some extrinsic source, since we are here concerned only with the natural dispositions of the human soul as regards what it has that is more noble and lofty. We are, then, investigating whether this noble part has a happiness that is proper to it or not. For since the animal part has its joys, its freedoms, its security and its unhappiness completely opposed to these, either that noble part likewise has an unhappiness and happiness befitting it, or it does not. If it does not, then there will be no spiritual and noble joys and the other lofty goods, and only a childish ignorance and a brutish irrationality can produce such ravings. [14] For it is more fitting that they exist *in* the greater and more noble than *in* the lesser and less noble, and in spiritual than in the bodily things. In accord with this view, only this more noble part will be unhappy and in no way capable of beatitude, because no power *is* capable of beatitude or of perfection except in terms of what is proper to it. But in accord with this view it does not have proper goods since there are no goods that are spiritual and befitting its nobility.

---

30. Cf. above, p. 34, ll. 5ff.

It is impossible that another power be made happy from the things which are suited to the animal part, since joy, or delight, lies only in what is suitable, and rest is found only in a suitable end, and perfection does not come from things of another sort, since perfection is the attainment of only those things which are potentially present in what can be perfected. This is also contrary to our observation and experience, since learned and wise men do not rejoice over bodily things and do not think that they are made happy because of them. Rather they turn aside from and avoid them as common and flee them as harmful and as impeding their happiness.

But since the moral philosophers have freed us from them and we have learned from observation that those things which their foolish lovers unwisely call goods make their owners unhappy or increase their unhappiness, we do not want to delay longer in an explanation of this sort. For our present purpose, we are satisfied with this one explanation, namely, that those who possess these bodily things either love them or do not love them. If they do not, it is clear that they are for them a burden and affliction, not a joy, and thus they not only do not add to their happiness, but detract from it. But if they do love them, they are joined and bound to them by love and, for [15] this reason, exposed to all the vicissitudes to which they are subject. For the lover and thing loved are, because of this union of love, necessarily related in this way. When the thing loved is affected, the lover is necessarily affected too, if the thing's transformation reaches him through apprehension. The lovers of such things admit that they share in how these things are affected by the very sad expressions of their language. They say that they have been destroyed, annihilated, beaten down, devastated, burned, and diminished when their possessions have been affected in one of these ways.[31] It is obvious, then, that things of this sort subject their lovers to as many kinds of unhappiness as the transformations to which the things are exposed. But if joys and other advantages <which they hope for from them were as many and as great as these disadvantages>,[32] they would add to happiness as much as they add to unhappiness, and the other way around. It is, then, the same as if no addition were made to either of them. But since there

---

31. In *De anima* ch. VI, pt. 2 (II, 137b), William is answering the claim that we should listen to the soul's testimony about itself, when one says, for example, "I am sick unto death, I am dying because of my illness." He explains that this is an improper mode of speaking; he explains the use of "I" to refer to the body as follows: "For every avaricious person speaking in the common idiom says when his house has been burned, that he has been burned, and when his vineyard has been destroyed by hail, he says that he has been destroyed by hail, and when his possessions are destroyed, he says that he has been destroyed. The reason for this is the joining together in strong love, and even a unity or a union of the avaricious with their possessions."

32. In w the preceding relative clause is omitted by reason of homoteleuton.

are more and greater disadvantages, it is obvious that they simply add so much to unhappiness and not to happiness.

It is also clear that the application to inferior and less noble things is a descent and a lowering, not an elevation. For this descent takes place in the manner of love which is a spontaneous subjection and servitude so that it is a worsening of the beings which are applied to things less noble and inferior to themselves. For every mingling is a separation from the other extreme, and thus this spiritual mingling – and that is what love is – is undoubtedly a separation from nobility and goodness and a drawing near to the ultimate commonness and lowness and, thus, misery.

Since we have elsewhere spoken about these matters and will often speak of them, let us set forth what every sound intellect accepts and say: Since a sense has its objects and things suited for it, by union with which [16] it is enlightened, perfected and delighted and since, in general, every animal power has its objects, it is likewise necessary that this spiritual power have its objects of apprehension that are noble and suitable, by the apprehension of which it is enlightened, perfected and delighted. For if nature has provided for the less noble powers in this way, how much the more has nature not neglected the more noble ones? They are, then, not left without objects that enlighten and perfect and delight them.[33]

Moreover, everything noble is naturally more suited to be applied to noble things than to less noble ones. But if this power is naturally suited to be applied only to these less noble, temporal and transitory things, it will not be noble at all, since nothing is created for what is less noble and more common than itself. But it is certain that all these things are more common and less noble. It does not exist, then, for the sake of these less noble things; thus it is not naturally suited to be perfected by them.[34]

---

33. In *De universo* II-I, c. 14 (I, 821b), William sets forth the reasons that Plato seems to have had or could have had for asserting the intelligible world. The first reason is that, as the testimony of the senses forces us to assert the sensible world, so the intellect leads us to assert the world of intelligibles. Second, he argues that intelligible objects cannot impress themselves upon our intellect unless they exist as they are understood. Third, he argues that, unless intelligibles exist as they are known, the senses would be more reliable witnesses than the intellect. Though William rejects the existence of the world of forms as distinct from God, he does view God as the higher book for the soul.

34. In *De anima* ch. VI, pt. 9 (II, 165b-166a) William says, "I want you to attend wisely and carefully to this root principle which is really the strongest root principle for establishing the immortality of human souls. It is this root principle which says that the Creator did not create (reading *creasse* for *curasse*) the human soul on account of the body or on account of the activities that it performs in it or through it . . . . The explanation of this root principle is the well known root principle among the philosophers that the more noble things were not created on account of the more common ones . . . ."

Moreover, the perfection of that which is more noble will itself be more noble, and the perfection of that which is more lofty will itself be more lofty, and the perfection of that which is spiritual will itself be spiritual, and the perfection of that which is separate from the body will be separate from the body. Since, then, this power is incorporeal and separate from the body, so that its activity neither takes place through the body nor depends upon the body, its perfection will likewise neither take place through the body nor depend upon the body. Hence, its perfection will be apart from the body, neither as a result of the body, nor through the body nor dependent upon the body in any way.

Moreover, its proper activity is strengthened in separation from the body and not as a result of the body, as can be seen in rapture and ecstasy. If, however, the strengthening of an activity attains the ultimate degree, it is the perfection of the power; if it does not attain the ultimate degree, it is an approximation [17] to its perfection. Hence, *it is* clear that separation from the body either brings it close to perfection or brings it into perfection itself. Thus it not only has life apart from the body, but also perfection, which is the glory of each power. It is ultimate, if the perfection itself is ultimate; it is lesser and of another order, if the perfection is less than ultimate.

Let us now continue what we began above.[35] Let us, then, say that this natural power has a natural desire for the happiness that is suitable and proper to it and a natural flight from, that is, a natural hatred and natural fear of its own unhappiness and misery. There is nothing in vain, nothing without a purpose among those things which occur naturally, but these motions are in vain and without a purpose if this evasion from misery is naturally impossible and if the attainment of such happiness is impossible. Hence, it is necessary that evasion from its misery and the attainment of its happiness is possible for this noble power. But if this attainment is not to be permanent, it will not be happiness or true immunity from misery. For whatever is subject to death is not happy; indeed, it is for that very reason wretched, because it is subject to extreme misery.

Permanence, however, cannot be a part of this happiness, because it is impossible that two contraries share a part.[36] Nor can it be the effect of this true and noble happiness, because, if that were the case, it would not coexist[37] <with its contrary, that is, with the misery opposed to it. It is necessary, then, that it be a disposition that must lie in the sub-

---

35. Cf. above, p. 34, ll. 5ff. and p. 35, ll. 9ff.

36. Bülow notes that the author must mean by "part" a specific difference, since two contraries can certainly share the same genus. For example, as black and white share the genus, color, so happiness and unhappiness could share permanence.

37. The text of w omits the remainder of this paragraph and skips to p. 45: "With regard then . . . ." The intervening material is found in w on p. 52 after the sentence: "We have, then, warded off . . . ."

ject of such happiness, since it does not follow it as its effect, or exist as a part of it, or accompany it with an essential accompaniment or correlative [18] connection. For in that case it would be impossible that permanence exist with the opposite misery. But it necessarily exists with it. Hence, it must be a preceding, quasi-material, disposition which happiness demands that there already be in the subject capable of receiving happiness. For a subject with the contrary disposition, that is, a mortal subject, is not able to receive such happiness.>[38]

Moreover, the life of the intellective power and its living in act[39] is nothing but its understanding in act, and it does not have this through the body or in dependence upon the body. <The living in act, then, of the intellect is not dependent upon the body,> because from the body's collapse it is rather raised up, from its weakness it is strengthened, and from its failure it is perfected, as is apparent in ecstasy and rapture. Life, then, – indeed, the perfection of its life – belongs to this noble power apart from and separate from the body.

Moreover, this rapture and this application to more noble *and higher* intelligibles is for this power either violent or voluntary, either natural or a matter of chance. It is impossible that it is a matter of chance, since this is its greatest <and most noble> perfection while it is in the body, and the human race is chiefly enlightened and ruled through this. For divine revelations and prophecies are what chiefly order human life, and every art and every wisdom yields to and is subjected to them. <Then every art and wisdom would yield to chance. But if it is natural, then withdrawal from the body and> application to noble incorporeal things is natural <to this noble power.> But nothing natural is harmful or deadly to that for which it is natural; <indeed it is salutary and helpful>. Therefore, to become separated from the body is salutary <and helpful> for this power. The same conclusion results if it is something voluntary [19] <of a natural or ordered will>. For everything that <proceeds from either of such wills>, is undoubtedly useful to the one who wills it. But that by which this power is generally helped, enlightened and perfected to

---

38. In *De anima* Ch. VI, pt. 17 (II, 172a), William takes up the objection "that immortality is not a natural disposition of the human soul, but something that accrues to it with happiness as if it were a part of it or something sharing it." He answers that "this happiness has as its contrary pure and universal misery, and by reason of their contrariety they are unmixed and do not share a part. Hence, they do not share the immortality of the subject. But they would share it if immortality were a part of happiness, since it is necessary that it be a part of the contrary misery which must be lasting, just as happiness is. For temporal misery and perpetual happiness can in no way be contraries, since all contraries must be equal or on a par." Hence, William holds that happiness and misery are pure and unmixed and, for that reason, permanence cannot be a part of happiness. He also argues that permanence or immortality is not the proper effect of happiness, but a natural disposition of the soul.

39. Bülow (p. 125) finds here in *uiuere in effectu* an allusion to Ibn Gabirol; cf. *Fons vitae* III, 23, p. 132.

this extent cannot be violent. For everything violent impedes and is harmful < to the nature for which it is violent >.

Moreover, it is clear that this noble power has two faces, of which
the one is enlightened < from above, that is, > by noble, incorporeal
things, < namely, those stripped from matter and its appendages, > and
the other can be enlightened from the lower side, that is, of bodily and
sensible things.[40] Or, it is the same power and the same face, but it is free
to turn itself to the side it wishes and to be enlightened or painted or
inscribed by whichever it wishes. < To whichever it turns, it turns to its
light and perfection. > But its more noble perfection and the more noble
light come from the higher. Hence, the more it turns to it < and unites
itself to it, the more it is perfected and > the more abundantly it is enlightened. It is certain that perfection and illumination separate it from non-
being and enlightens its very being itself. Conversion, then, to the things
which are above it perfects and enlightens this noble power. But it is clear
that this conversion separates it from the body and from bodily things and
unites it to spiritual things that are stripped from matter and separated
from the body. It ought, then, to be obvious that this power not only does
not depend upon the body, but is rendered obscure and impeded by it and
by its application to it.

Moreover, it is certain that, after some powerful object of the
senses has been sensed, [20] it leaves the sense weaker for sensing other
things. And with a powerful object of the intellect, the opposite is the
case, because it leaves the intellect stronger for understanding other
things. < If the application or union of something helps the activity, it is
necessary that a greater application or union help it more, unless the
activity has a mean or harmony,[41] such as there is in the activities of the

---

40. Bülow (p. 126) points out that Gundissalinus speaks of two faces of the human mind.
"Thus when the human mind turns its superior face, that is, the power of intelligence,
toward the contemplation of God, it is illumined from that side and seems bright to itself,
because it gazes upon itself or God without any intervening phantasm, but with its face
unveiled. But when it lowers itself through the inferior power, namely, knowledge, to
understand and arrange sensible things, it becomes dark as a result and does not see itself,
because it cannot at the same time attend to itself and other things, to earthly things and
eternal things, . . ." (De anima, ed. J. T. Muckle, Mediaeval Studies 2 [1940] 102). Bülow
also cites Algazali's Liber philosophiae, ed. Petrus Liechtensteyn (Venice, 1506), tr. 4, ch. V:
"But the human soul has two faces, the one toward the superior part, which is a superior
vastness, because from it it acquires the sciences, and it has only a speculative function with
respect to that part from which it must always be receptive, and the other face toward the
lower part, namely, for ruling the body."
41. In De anima ch. VI, pt. 4 (II, 160a), William reports, "Aristotle says that a harmony is
a certain mean. Just as in all harmonies the pleasing quality is destroyed by every sensible
decrease or excess of sharpness or graveness, and it becomes a dissonance that offends the
ear . . . , so in the disposition of one's members if someone has more or less than the due
balance, the operation which is to be performed through them is injured or impeded. For
this reason Aristotle says that extremes destroy a sense." Cf. Aristotle, De anima II, 11,
424a4-6.

senses. A greater application to sensible things or to objects that are more sensible either harms or destroys them altogether. But just the opposite is true with the intellect, because its application or union with more powerful objects of the intellect helps and perfects its activity. But if the greater and stronger application of something helps or perfects the activity, it is impossible that it harm or destroy the essence of the power, whose activity it naturally helps and perfects.>[42] It is impossible, then, that the essence of this noble power be injured as a result of its applications to things that are powerful objects of the intellect that are bare, stripped and separated from matter; indeed, it is necessary that it be helped by its union with them and that it be helped the more in proportion to the strength of its union with them. But it is certain that this sort of union, namely, the strongest, separates it entirely and removes it from the senses and the body. And thus it is clear that what naturally preserves and perfects this power separates it from the body. Separation, then, from the body is a consequence of its preservation and perfection, not a cause or occasion of its destruction or of its injury.

Moreover, it is clear that this power does not have in the body an organ for its operation. Although from an injury to the middle compartment of the head the operation of this power seems to be impeded or completely destroyed, still it is clear that [21] this impedes or destroys only the operation it has from below, that is, from the side of sensible things.[43] For its representation of the sensible forms is like another book, a book that the imaginative power offers or presents to it.[44] Since, then, it

---

42. Cf. Aristotle, *De anima* III, 4, 429a29-429b4. In *De anima* V, 2, p. 97, Avicenna says in reference to knowing powers that use an organ, "But those things which are strong and difficult to apprehend weaken and sometimes destroy the organs so that afterwards they do not apprehend weaker objects than those, because the modification from the difficult object penetrated too deeply. Such is the disposition of a sense which difficult and constant objects of the senses weaken and at times destroy. Thus brilliance weakens and destroys sight, and a great clap of thunder weakens or destroys hearing so that, after apprehending a difficult object, it cannot apprehend a weak one. For one who looks at too much brightness does not see a weaker light along with it or soon afterward, and one who hears a very loud sound does not hear a softer one along with it or after it, and one who tastes something too sweet does not sense something less sweet after it. In the case of an intelligible object just the opposite is the case. For the frequency of its action and of the formation of concepts which are difficult acquires for it the power of afterwards apprehending more easily what is weaker than those objects . . . ."

43. William, following Avicenna, rejects any bodily organ for the intellective power. Nonetheless, the middle compartment of the brain is the organ of the imaginative power and becomes for the intellect a book inscribed by and representing the sensible world. For a summary of the localization of the internal senses among the Arabian philosophers, cf. Klubertanz, pp. 122-123.

44. In *De anima* ch. VII, pt. 6 (II, 211b) William says that "in accord with Christian doctrine . . . we must state that the human soul is naturally established and ordered, as if on the horizon of two worlds. One of these worlds is for it the sensible world . . . , but the other is the Creator himself as the exemplar and mirror . . . . And for this reason the Creator himself is the natural and proper book of the human intellect . . . ."

cannot abstract or strip these forms from particular conditions because of
the disturbance or injury of the middle compartment of the head, into
which they pass from the imaginative power, though more stripped and
abstracted from matter, this noble power is prevented from seeing and
reading them. This is due to the fact that the middle compartment, which
<through the imaginative power> ought to become like a book for it by
means of such an inscription as we mentioned, is by reason of injury from
an infection or from a wound unsuited to be inscribed by the imaginative
power. Hence, this power is prevented from the reading <that it would do
in such a book,> that is, it is prevented from understanding and from reasoning about sensible things which come to it in no other way.

But is it prevented <from its illumination which is from above
and> from its reading in its more noble book and from the illumination
which comes to it from the first light or from the intermediate lights,
which are called holy angels?[45] It is certain that it is not prevented from
reading this nobler book, and this is clearly seen in those suffering from
melancholy, *and delirious persons* who, though they are prevented from
reasoning about these sensible things, still at times see much concerning
lofty things and foretell the future, as if they were prophesying.[46] In this
case, then, it is obvious that the book of reason inscribed by sensible
things has been taken away from them, but the higher noble book is in the
meantime unveiled and opened for them. For it does not seem to be
always in contact with our reason or intelligence, [22] but at times <the
intelligence is applied to it – or> it is applied to our intellective
power – and at times it becomes far removed from it. We have to discuss
and explain elsewhere what is the reason for this.[47] It is clear from this
that, <if> the destruction of that part <of the human body> does not
destroy or extinguish this power, I mean, the part <through which and>
in which it especially seems to be active, that is, in the middle compartment of the head *or of the brain*, <much less will the destruction of the
rest destroy it. For if its more noble activity is then especially vigorous,
when that part is harmed or destroyed, insofar as it was helping this

---

45. William links reading (*legere*) with understanding (*intelligere*) and thinks of what we
understand as a book – either the book of this universe or the book that is God. The intermediate lights, which William calls the holy angels, are remnants of the separate
intelligences emanated by the first cause, the last of which was the agent intelligence or
"giver of forms." William rejected the Avicennian doctrine of an agent intelligence
because, as the source of our being, knowledge, and happiness, it had usurped the role of
God. Cf. *De anima* ch. V, pt. 2 (II, 112b).

46. In *De anima* ch. VI, pt. 5 (II, 161a), William says, "Moreover, how many souls and
what great souls we have seen grow strong and be strengthened in respect of their principal
powers and to be capable of things in the gravest illnesses of their bodies which they were
not capable of in good health."

47. William speaks of prophetic revelation as a book that opens and closes itself, disclos-
ing as it wills certain pages or words to whomever it wills (cf. *De anima* ch. VII, pt. 6, II,
211b-212a).

power – as was clear in the previous example of melancholy persons who otherwise do not prophesy at all, but do prophesy when they are in the grip of this illness, then it is clear that this power lives in a more lofty and noble manner when this portion of its body is dead for it. Nothing then is lost from the death of the rest of the body in terms of what is needed for being and for its more noble activity. > [48]

Moreover, every essence that naturally tends toward and naturally rests only in the place in which corruption or death does not touch it is naturally incorruptible and immortal. [49] For everything that is sought naturally, <that is, by a natural motion,> is natural to what seeks it. But <if it is true that> this power seeks by a natural <motion of its own, which is flight or> desire, <such> a place <or state> where neither corruption nor death can touch it, such a place or state, then, is natural to it and naturally owed to it. <And for this reason all the dispositions natural to that place or state are natural and owed to it and, hence, incorruptibility and immortality,> and thus it is <naturally> immune from death and corruption. For example, fire in its natural place, which is the vault of the lunar heaven, is incorruptible, <because [23] corruption would in no way reach to that place, since incorruptibility would be one of the conditions and consequences of that place. But it is here both generable and corruptible> in terms of the condition of its place. For every place beneath the lunar heaven is a place of generation and corruption, because it is a place of conflict <and of action and being acted upon, from which all generation and corruption arises.> Because, then, the place or state of separated immaterial things stripped from matter is far removed from motion and change, because it is far from matter and the appendages of matter, it is obvious that this noble power is naturally immune from corruption and free from death, <just as every essence which is naturally moved toward the place where all things are subject to or liable to corruption indicates by its own motion and inclination and by the region it seeks that it is subject and liable to corruption>. [50]

But if someone says that the human soul is naturally moved toward the body, he says this equivocally. For it is not moved to the body so that it might rest in it or so that it might be perfected by it, but rather so that it might perfect the body and use it to acquire for itself some of its

---

48. In w the preceding bracketed text is reduced to: But this is confirmed by the previously mentioned example, namely, that delirious persons prophesy in the grip of their disease and not otherwise.

49. In *De anima* ch. VII, pt. 13 (II, 168b), William argues as follows: "Moreover, everything which is moved toward the region to which corruption and death do not reach, I mean: everything that is moved by a natural motion or intention of its nature, has the power and potency of reaching that place."

50. Instead of the preceding bracketed text, w continues as follows: For everything that is moved here below is subject to corruption.

secondary perfections insofar as it is helped by organs <of the senses> or by sensible things. That is not the way we understand the human soul to be moved toward what is spiritual and noble above it, indeed as toward the place of its ultimate perfection and to its most noble state. Heaven forbid that, in terms of that sublime and noble power it has, the human soul should seek to rest in sensible things or to be perfected by them. Just so, on the contrary, [24] the lower power, namely, the animal or earthly one, <which is its lowest power>, does not seek to rest or be perfected in sublime things, <that is, in spiritual things that are stripped and separated from matter>. Still we do not deny that it is helped to some extent <with respect to some perfection of itself by sensible things and even by the senses which it uses> for the acquisition of many areas of knowledge and for the accomplishment of many activities.

Moreover, every power entirely separated from the body is necessarily incorruptible by the corruption of the body <and not mortal by its death.>[51] <And likewise every power entirely united to a body and entirely impressed upon the body is necessarily mortal and corruptible by the death and corruption of the body. Or let us put it this way: every power entirely separate and entirely independent of the body is immortal and incorruptible by the death and corruption of the body, and every power, on the other hand, entirely in the body and entirely dependent upon it is necessarily mortal and corruptible by the death and corruption of the body. That, then, which holds an intermediate position between the first pair of extremes will hold an intermediate position between the last pair. As examples of all these>[52] the holy angels are entirely separate and entirely independent of bodies, and the vegetative and sensitive souls are entirely impressed upon bodies and dependent upon them. But the human soul is an example of something in between; it is partly impressed upon the body and partly dependent upon it, namely, with respect to the powers it shares with the sensitive and vegetative soul, but it is partly separate and abstracted <and not dependent upon the body>, that is, in terms of <its sublime and noble powers which> it shares with the holy angels that are stripped of what is contrary to them. By an *essential* proportion, [25] then, some of its powers are immortal, some are mortal. And this is what we have been searching after. For it is not contrary to the piety or the truth of the faith that sight or hearing or some other sense is mortal and subject to extinction, but that the human mind, as human, is

---

51. The text of w ends the previous sentence with: and the opposite is true as well.

52. The following sentence from w is omitted in g: It follows that there is something in between and of an intermediate disposition between the extremes.

mortal, that is, undoubtedly, contrary to the true and pious faith.[53] That, then, which is chief and most noble in the human soul is wholly immortal.

But someone might object that *it is mortal, because,* if part is mortal or corruptible, then the whole is. For how is a home to be incorruptible if its wall is corruptible? We answer to this that sight is not corruptible except in terms of what it has from the body, and we can call this the assistance from the modifications it undergoes or the suitability of the organ for receiving changes from visible things. But the power of judging depends entirely upon the essence of the mind which is not at all dependent upon the body. In the animal soul sight depends upon the body for two reasons. For it depends upon the body both in terms of what it has from the body and in terms of what it has from the essence of the animal soul. And this is the reason that it depends upon the body. The reason < for this sort of difference > is that the human soul has the animal powers as secondary, and thus it is not itself dependent upon them in terms of what it has that is most important. Indeed, just the opposite is the case: The secondary powers depend upon the principal ones in this way, namely, that they exist for the sake of them. < And it is universally true that > in every subject < all the secondary and > the less noble things exist for the sake of the important and more noble ones. [26] With regard, then, to what the animal powers have as a result of the body, < they depend on the body to that extent; as regards the root principles of judging, they do not depend upon the body, >[54] because the root principles themselves depend upon the essence of the soul as rays stretched forth from its luminosity. But the soul need not depend upon the body on account of its secondary and less noble elements, since insofar as they depend upon the body, they are not essential to the soul. They are essential to it only in terms of the root principles of judging.[55] It is more fitting, however, that those things which are important and noble draw the secondary and less noble toward their strength than that the less noble draw the noble ones to their weakness. Thus it is entirely fitting that the rays follow the light and that, in general, an effect follows the cause, not that

---

53. William uses the expressions "piety or the truth of the faith" and "the true and pious faith." Yet there is nothing in his discussion of immortality that even hints at the doctrine of the resurrection of the body. This absence may be a further influence of an Arabian philosophical source upon his thought. For evidence of such an Avicennian influence on William's eschatology, cf. Alan E. Bernstein, "Estoteric Theology: William of Auvergne on the Fires of Hell and Purgatory," *Speculum* 57 (1982) 509-531.

54. The immediately preceding bracketed text was omitted in w by homoteleuton.

55. In *De anima* ch. III, pt. 7 (II, 93a-b), William explains that the sense powers are unable to correct their errors: "it is not their task to judge or examine this error." He later adds that "it is clear that the senses or sensible powers are subject to this power [the intellect] as to its judge and corrector by the law and order of nature . . . ." He claims that without this corrective power the senses would have "neither a certain message nor a fixed and certain root."

the effect draws the cause to itself and after itself. We say all this so that our understanding might be clearer about our having said that the animal powers depend upon the body and are corruptible, according to the mind of the philosophers. It is apparent, then, that the human soul is midway between the animal souls and the angelic substances that are stripped from matter and are spiritual. And thus it is, as we said, necessarily in between in terms of the dispositions of mortality and immortality with the sort of mediateness that we have determined.

Moreover, what is destructible can be destroyed in only one of these ways: It is destroyed either through the division of its form from its matter. This can happen only in one of these ways: Either with the form remaining, as we have said happens in the case of man who is destroyed in this way in death. Death is the division of form from matter, that is, of the soul from the body, <but his form, that is, his soul remains, as we have said. [27] Or>⁵⁶ that which is destroyed <is destroyed> by the division of form from matter with the form itself destroyed. This destruction is what is called corruption in the proper sense. Or, it is destroyed by the division of its integral parts, just as a house is when its parts, that is, the wood and the stones, are separated from one another. Or, it is destroyed when the essence of what sustains it is destroyed, or it is destroyed by the removal of its cause. Thus wine perishes or is destroyed when the vessel holding it is destroyed, and things in a body are destroyed when the body is destroyed, or the daylight is destroyed when the sun is withdrawn. That is, one thing is destroyed by the destruction of another in two ways: either, because it is its cause as the present sun is for the daylight, or because it is its carrier or sustainer, as matter is for form, or a vessel for a liquid. Some forms depend upon the matters in which they are, or upon their subjects.

Someone might say that there is a fifth manner of destruction, namely, a proper failing, such as aging or decay. <But his objection comes to nothing, for if aging and decay>⁵⁷ would not lead to any of the four manners of destruction, they would in no way destroy anything. For if the union of form with matter and the integrity and union of the parts are preserved, if the presence of the cause is preserved, and if the essence of what sustains it is also preserved, the thing is necessarily preserved. But it is certain that aging leads to the division of the soul and body and that decay is the division of form from matter and the destruction of the form itself. If he says that some things perish through their failing alone and fail by a certain weakness of their essence, he necessarily has to determine the mode of failure. If everything that perishes perishes only through the weakness of its essence, by reason of which it is in itself weak and [28]

---

56. The preceding bracketed text was omitted in w by homoteleuton.
57. The preceding bracketed text was omitted in w by homoteleuton.

without the strength to last *forever*, it is obvious that everything created is of this sort, that is, infirm and weak in itself and without the strength to last in terms of what it has in itself.[58] If each thing has this infirmity, none of those things which are will last, because that cause of not lasting is found in all things. But we see that many things last, some longer than others, and some perish more rapidly. What, then, will be the reason for this except that a proper infirmity or weakness does not of itself destroy any of those things which are, unless it is helped in one of the manners we have mentioned or it is impeded by their contraries?

There remains, then, for us to inquire whether one of the manners of destruction that we mentioned can fit the human soul, in terms of our inquiry about it here. And it is clear that it cannot be destroyed in the first way, because it is pure form and an immaterial substance that is not in itself composed with the sort of composition that arises from matter and form.[59]

Or someone might at this point say that it is composed from matter and form. To this we say that its form is incorruptible, because it does not have a contrary by which it might be corrupted or something divisive by which it might be divided or something that supports it by whose removal it might be destroyed. For the form of the intellective power cannot have a contrary. <If it had a contrary,> it would not be able to receive its contrary or a likeness of it, just as whiteness is not able to receive blackness or a likeness of [29] blackness or of one of the intermediate *colors*.[60] Since the intellective power cannot understand anything unless there is present to it either the thing itself or its likeness, it is clear

---

58. In *The Trinity* ch. VI, p. 81, while listing the names of created being, William says, "Dependent being (*esse*) is that which for its own part falls back into non-being (*non esse*); that it stands firm is due to another." William's point here is that every created being has the defectibility to which the objection points. Hence, if some beings last – and some last longer than others –, this proper weakness does not of itself explain the perishing of anything. William's problem is one for any philosopher who holds that the human soul is immortal and yet dependent upon the first cause for its being. In *De anima* ch. V, pt. 24 (II, 151a), William says, "The proper and natural defectibility is sufficient for each creature's falling back into the non-being from which it has been drawn into being by the Creator. No one of them remains and persists in being unless the Creator holds and conserves it in being, overcoming its potentiality by his own actuality applied to it by the choice of his excellent will alone." In *De anima* ch. VI, pt. 8 (II, 164a-b), William deals with the natural defectibility of the soul.

59. The immateriality of the soul is one of the key points on which the author differs from the Augustinian tradition as well as from Ibn Gabirol. The Augustinian tradition had maintained that matter, as the principle of mutability, was present in all creatures and distinguished between corporeal and spiritual matter. It is perhaps even more significant that the text rejects universal hylomorphism – a doctrine that Gundissalinus had adopted from Avicebron – and thus provides some internal evidence that *De immortalitate animae* is not the work of Gundissalinus.

60. The argument here is that corruption takes place through the loss of one form and the acquisition of a contrary form. But the intellective power has no contrary form, since it can receive all forms. Cf. Aristotle, *De anima* III, 4, 429a19-22.

it cannot understand its contrary and, therefore, cannot have a contrary. For everything that is proximate to it is naturally intelligible to it, since much greater and loftier things are also intelligible for it. Besides, this objection states only that the intellective power has a contrary, and thus it states that there is something that is not intelligible to it. This statement is *not an explanation, but* madness, and hence we should not argue against it further: one cannot assert the existence of what is unintelligible.[61]

Moreover, as sight has no contrary from among the visible forms, so the intellect has none from among the intelligible forms, and on this point it is not necessary for us to produce a proof, since there is the same reason in both cases. It is, then, not destructible by the division of form from matter, since its form cannot have a contrary, but is to all the intelligible forms, <as hyle[62] is to all visible ones.> Hence, as the latter is incorruptible by bodily corruption, so the former is incorruptible by spiritual corruption, *and for this reason* is all the more <incorruptible by bodily corruption>, since bodily corruption cannot touch it because of its lofty nature. For if this sort of corruption does not touch the hyle of bodies, much less will it touch what is above it. But the intellect seems unintelligible on this account if it is related to all bodily and spiritual forms by its ability to receive them[63] and by its separateness from them. [30] For just as hyle is to bodily ones, *the intellect is to spiritual ones*. And <it has seemed to many that,> just as sight is invisible, <and so on regarding the other senses,> so the intellect is unintelligible.

If someone asks how sight can be corrupted by visible forms, we answer that sight is a harmony as regards its organ, and its power is partially in the organ. For this reason it is necessarily destroyed by the destruction of that organ to the extent that it depends upon it. But the organ of sight is destroyed by things that exceed its harmony, that is, by powerful objects of sight. Just the opposite is the case with the intellect, since the intellect does not have a determinate part in the body that is its organ, and it is strengthened and grows strong as a result of powerful objects of the intellect. How would an intelligible form, that might by its action destroy the intellect, act upon it except by impressing upon it its likeness and likening it to itself? But the more it could do this, the more intelligible it would be and, for that reason, the more it would strengthen it. Thus it is not only not destroyed in this way, but is even strengthened.

---

61. To say that the intellective power has a contrary is to say that there is something that is unintelligible. But to know that it is unintelligible involves knowing something about it.

62. William has transliterated the Greek term for matter.

63. Cf. Aristotle, *De anima* III, 4, 429b30-31: "The mind is potentially whatever is thinkable, though actually it is nothing until it has thought . . . ." Cf. also *De anima* III, 5, 430a14-15: "And the intellect is . . . what it is by virtue of becoming all things." Cf. also 429a15-20.

Moreover, the more intelligible something is, the more it is able to act upon the intellect and the more it is able to liken it to itself or unite it *to itself*. This is a certain indication of the powerfulness of the action and of the strength of the acting power, that is, of the powerfulness of the transformation, whose perfection is the ultimate likening to the agent. Therefore, the greater the likening is, the more powerful will be the action, and the stronger the power acting upon what is acted upon. Hence, it is clear that the more powerful objects of the intellect have a more powerful and stronger action on the intellect. But everything that cannot be injured by the more powerful agents [31] cannot be injured for even better reasons by what acts less and more weakly. Hence, because the intellective power is strengthened, not merely not injured, by the objects of the intellect no matter how powerful they are, it is clear that it can be injured by the action of none of them, unless someone were to say that, as sight can be injured by things not objects of sight, so by the injury of its organ, the intellect can be injured by things that are not intelligible.[64] But this is clearly false, both because the intellect does not have an organ in the body and because what is not intelligible does not have a form and is not a form. But all action arises from form, and therefore it is impossible that what is not intelligible act upon it.

But if someone says that the intellect is not form at all, <and does not have a form>,[65] and it is, therefore, impossible that it act, we answer that the intellect in itself, in its being and in its species, is form. Just as clear liquid or visible air[66] is in its being something formed and yet somehow material with respect to light and color, so the intellect is to all intelligibles which are outside of it. Insofar as it is material, it does not act in this way, that is, by its essence, but through a form, when it has grasped it. Through the form the intellect is active just as the artisan acts through the seal by which the material of the artifact is sealed from the outside.

That it is not destructible by the division of integral parts will be clear from the fact that the intellect is necessarily without parts.[67] We render this certain as follows. If it had parts, it would not, as a whole, be

---

64. Sight can be injured not merely by a visible object that is too strong, e.g., a very bright light, but also by an unseen or invisible object, e.g., a blow to the head.

65. Bülow notes that Ibn Gabirol's student poses a similar objection: "I have seen wise men agree on this point, namely, that the intelligence does not have a form that is proper to it. And they have given an account of this, saying that, if the intelligence had its own form, that form would prevent the apprehension of all other forms besides itself" (*Fons vitae* V, 16, p. 286). As Bülow notes, Ibn Gibirol's response differs from that which we have here. The basis of the objection goes back to Aristotle's *De anima* III, 4, 429a19-23.

66. Bülow takes this as referring to the transparent fluid of the eye and the animal spirits.

67. William uses the term *"impartibilis"* which I have translated as "indivisible" or "without parts." In his *De Anima*, William argues extensively against any sort of parts or distinct potencies in the soul. Cf. *De anima* ch. II, pts. 10 and 11 (II, 80a-82a) and ch. III, pt. 2 (II, 87b-88b) and ch. II, pt. 6 (II, 91a-93a).

acted upon at one time, or be acted upon by a whole at one time, but by one part after another, as though a part of what is understood [32] would enter the intellect after another part, and not the whole at once. And from this it follows that something continuous and with parts could only be understood continuously and part by part and that a part could only be understood in a part of a time, and the whole only in the whole of a time, and that in his knowing the knower follows the time of the passing of the syllables and the elements or letters and understands them in a continuous transition and not instantaneously. But everyone who knows is aware of the opposite in himself.[68]

Moreover, the intellect is aware that it understands as a whole as often as it understands; it is itself a witness that it is never the case that a part of itself understands, while another part does not, because the whole intellect understands at once and not one part of it before another. Because this takes place before and in the intellect, we should take its word alone about this. For as one intellect understands, so every intellect does, < – for this belongs to its nature – >, and thus the manner of understanding will be the same for all of them, just as the manner of seeing is the same for all. Hence, what one intellect knows within itself concerning the manner of understanding, all intellects necessarily find <with themselves and> in themselves. All who intellectually attend to this find that

---

68. In *De anima* ch. II, pt. 10 (II, 80a-b) William develops a similar argument. "Having settled these matters I will free myself and you from the promise I made in the previous pages that I would bring you to know by the testimony of each intelligent soul its incorporeity and indivisibility. I say, then, that every intelligent soul also understands that it understands. Likewise, it knows that it understands, and understands that it knows this. For it understands that its act of understanding exists and is present to it or in it. And if you asked it whether its act of understanding was in a part of it or in the whole, it would have to answer that it is in the whole. Otherwise, it would understand that only a part of itself understands and not itself, just as a man seeing himself says that it is himself only in a certain respect, but he will not say that it is himself without qualification. But every soul says that it understands without qualification when it looks at itself in thought; it cannot see that a part of it understands and a part does not understand. It is necessary, then, that the whole of it understand. Because the act of understanding is indivisible into parts of a continuum, it is necessary that the subject in which it is be indivisible essentially and without qualification. That which truly and properly understands is the true and proper subject of the act of understanding. Because the human soul truly and properly understands, it is clear that it is the true, proper and indivisible subject of the disposition which is the act of understanding. It is, then, necessary that it be indivisible and, for that reason, incorporeal, since it has already been explained to you in Aristotle and in many others that every body is infinitely divisible."

"Moreover, to understand is an instantaneous act and it is completed in an instant, and each person experiences this internally before himself and in himself. For when your soul understands man in the universal, it understands the whole at once, not a part after a part, since it does not then think of the part or parts of man. For this reason, what understands it is without parts and indivisible; it is accomplished in an instant. But nothing with parts that are continuous receives a disposition in an instant, but receives it part after part, until that change of it is accomplished. Otherwise, the continuum would be changed in terms of the whole of itself in an instant. But this is something impossible."

hearing takes place continuously, but that understanding is instantaneous. But, since understanding takes place only through a change of the intellect, if the intellect had parts and were also continuous, it would be impossible to understand instantaneously, since it has been explained elsewhere that it is impossible for something continuous to be changed instantaneously. It remains then that the intellect is without parts and not continuous, and it is, therefore, indestructible by the division of its parts, since it does not have parts of that kind.[69]

It is clear, then, that the intellect is indestructible by all manners of destruction. For it is not possible that something be destroyed save by the divison of its form from matter or by the division [33] of its integral parts or by the destruction of what bears and sustains it,[70] which manners of destruction we have already removed, or by the withdrawal of the efficient cause which is the last manner, as, for example, the daylight is destroyed by the withdrawal of the sun and the body by the withdrawal of the soul.

But this cannot happen in the human soul. For it is clear that it is by its nature in continuity with the first cause, or with what is in continuity with it.[71] This is apparent from the fact that the activities of the first cause continuously flow forth upon natural things and upon all the things that nature has prepared, as is the case with being and life. And it is impossible that, when the matter has been prepared by nature, there not flow forth from the first cause either life or another form – and what is more, the soul is necessarily infused, when the seed has been prepared.[72] This, then, is a clear indication of the continuity or connection of nature to the first cause. But connection arises only from nearness, and things that are

---

69. This argument seems to have its ultimate source in Plotinus. Cf. *Ennead* V,3,1, where Plotinus asks whether that which thinks itself has to be complex so that it may by one of its parts contemplate the rest. Plotinus argues in V,3,5 that self-knowledge does not mean that the knower sees himself with another part of himself so that one part sees and the other part is seen. In that way the knower would "not know himself completely or as a whole." Hence, in V,3,6 he concludes that "intellect and intellection are one; and it thinks as a whole with the whole of itself, not one part of itself with another." Cf. *Plotinus*, with an English translation by A. H. Armstrong. Vol. V. (Cambridge, MA: Harvard University Press, 1984), pp. 73, 85 and 89. In *De trinitate* X,iii,5-iv,6 (*CC* L, 317-319), St. Augustine takes up much the same line of argumentation that in self-knowledge the whole self knows the whole of itself, not a part of itself by a part. William develops the argument further and in a different direction than either Plotinus or Augustine.

70. It is not clear where in this argument William explicitly rules out the destruction of the soul by the removal of what sustains it, i.e., presumably by the removal of the body. He mentions this point on p. 47 in passing. Earlier, of course, he showed that the human soul did not depend upon the body.

71. The text leaves open the possibility of some intermediate cause, such as the agent intelligence of the Arabian philosophers, which would mediate the causality of the first cause. Later William adamantly rejects any such role for the agent intelligence. Cf. *De anima* ch. V, pt. 2 (II, 112b).

72. This is good Avicennian doctrine, but it seems to imply that the first cause does not act freely. Cf. Avicenna, *De anima* VI, ch. xii.

closer are necessarily more connected to the same thing. For to the extent
the human soul is higher than nature, < to that extent it is more connected
to the highest.[73] To the extent it is higher, and thus nearer than nature, >
to that extent it is nearer to the highest. Since the outpourings of the highest are ordered in accord with the order of nearness to it, they are necessarily greater and more continuous upon those things which are nearer to
the first cause than upon the more remote ones, and if they cannot cease
with regard to the more remote, much less can they cease with regard to
the nearer. And thus the influxes [34] of life and other natural
outpourings are much more unceasing and continuous upon the rational
soul than upon nature. It is obvious, then, that the rational soul cannot die
in this last manner.

Someone might say that it follows from this that the sensitive soul
is also immortal and unfailing. But we have already given our answer to
these objections in what went before where we said that it depends in all
its powers upon the body,[74] and this is the reason that it dies with the
death of the body.

It does not, then, die or fail by reason of the failure of the influx
of life into it from the first and universal source of life.

We have, then, warded off all modes of corruption and failure
from the rational soul with regard to what it has that is lofty, noble and
divine.[75]

We shall try to explain its immortality in another way. We will
say, then, that a sense is not applied to things that are sensed without its
being likened to them. Thus touch is not applied to what is hot without
becoming hot, and sight to what is bright without being illumined. But the
intellect behaves in the opposite manner in this respect.[76] < For when we
sense something hot we necessarily become hot, and when we sense
something bright we are necessarily illumined, but when we understand
something hot we do not in any way become hot, nor do we in any way
become colored when we understand a color. There is no modification

---

73. Cf. the Prologue to the *De anima* (II, 65a) where William expresses him amazement
at those philosophers who have treated the human soul in natural philosophy. He says, "I
do not think that they held the same thing regarding that knowledge which directly and
essentially concerns the human soul. For its more noble and lofty dispositions which I
intend to examine and explain in this science are above nature and above all natural real-
ities."

74. Cf. above pp. 44-46.

75. In w there follows at this point the section that is found earlier in g, beginning on p.
41: "Moreover, the life of this intellective power . . . ," and running until p. 45, ". . . for the
sake of the important and more noble ones."

76. The text of w contains the following instead of the next four sentences: For when it
understands something, it is not called by the name of what it understands. For nothing is
in the intellect derived from the things understood except perhaps the act of understanding, as in the case of sensible things there is the act of sensing. And thus it is clear that the
intellect is not affected by the intelligible thing or things.

except by the agent's application to or union with what is modified, and there is no more fitting union, no more powerful application of the intellect to intelligible or sensible things than the very understanding of them. It is the same in the case in sensation, because there is no greater or more powerful application of them to the sense than the sensing of them. Hence, it is clear that the intellect cannot naturally be modified [35] or at least cannot be harmed by sensible objects and, hence, cannot be burned or cut.>

Moreover, besides this there is another difference <between sense and intellect> that we mentioned above,[77] namely, <that the more some things are sensible, the more they harm the sense, but> the more the objects of the intellect are powerfully intelligible, the more they delight and strengthen the intellect. <If, then, the intellect can be modified by these things, it can only be strengthened and delighted by them.>[78]

Moreover, it is clear that, to the extent that the intellective power understands more and greater things and does so more often, to that extent it is freer and more capable and stronger in terms of understanding.[79] Just the opposite is the case with a sense. It is clear, then, that it does not have an end in its activity; for no power can do anything beyond its end. But every power that does not have an end in its activity does not have an end in time. The intellective power, then, does not have an end in time. For every power with an endless activity lasts for an endless time. An endless activity cannot be completed in a finite time. If, then, it is true that its activity does not have an end beyond which it cannot go <–for example, if it could not go beyond a certain number of things that it understands or a certain amount of them–because it does not have an end of this sort, it is clear that its activity does not have an end. Hence, for much better reasons the power does not have an end. But if a power is naturally without an end in its activity, for much better reasons it will not have an end in its duration. This is obvious in a moving power. If it does not have a limit or an end in its activity, that is, in moving, it will in no way have a limit or end in its being or duration. [36] For it is necessary that

---

77. Cf. above, pp. 40-41.

78. The text of w has only the following instead of the previous sentence: and thus it is not subject to being changed.

79. The rest of this paragraph is considerably shorter in w; it reads: It is clear then that it does not have an end to its activity. But every power with an endless activity lasts for an endless time. Every power which does not have an end in its activity does not have an end in time. For an endless activity cannot be completed in time. If then it is true that its activity does not have an end beyond which it cannot go, as the same power does not have an end in its activity, so it does not have an end in its essence. And this is clear in a moving power that does not have an end in its movement; thus it has an end neither in acting nor in enduring.

the cause be in every way greater in actuality, and thus, if the activity does not naturally have an end, neither does the power.>

But if someone says that <any activity of the intellect, that is, any act of understanding, is finite, but its act of understanding without qualification is endless, he says nothing that presents an objection. For the intellective power does not exist for the sake of a particular act of understanding, but for the sake of the act of understanding without qualification, and the particular act of understanding is in a sense like a part of that which is the act of understanding without qualification. Just as, then, any revolution of the heavens or any motion of them is finite in terms of time, but the motion of the heavens without qualification is not, thereby, finite, nor are their revolutions without qualification able to be counted, even though any of them can be counted, so it is in the case both of the intellective power and of its activity which can be called its activity without qualification.[80] For if the power that moves the first heaven or anything else has the extent and frequency of its motion determined and has this determined naturally, both it and its activity would necessarily be finite with respect to time. But because the contrary is the case, both of them are necessarily endless with respect to time. And, therefore, it must likewise be this way in the case of the intellective power.>[81]

But if someone says that this power has its end in the first light, because beyond it there is nothing for it to understand <or seek to know>, what we are aiming at presents no objection to him, for it is clear that this end is endless, <and for this reason he does not say that the activity of the intellective power is brought to an end in it>.

[37] It is even necessary, as a consequence of this, that the intellective power be immortal. For if its ultimate rest and perfection lies in life itself, indeed in the very source of life, where neither death nor failure draws near, it is clear that the human mind naturally tends toward

---

80. Bülow points to this text to show that the author explicitly rejects the eternal motion of the heavens and thus disagrees with Avicebron. Cf. Bülow, p. 103, and *Fons vitae* III, 51, p. 153, 13. As I read the text, it says that any particular motion of the heavens is finite, but the motion of the heavens without qualification is infinite. Just below the author says that the power that moves the first heaven or any thing else does not have the extent or frequency of its motion naturally determined; rather, both it and its activity are endless with respect to time. It is striking that this passage is omitted from the text which Bülow attributed to William, though that text is most probably a later revision of William's earlier version. If that is correct, then William came to reject the doctrine of the eternity of the world between writing the first version and his *De universo* which Kramp dates as 1231-1236. Cf. my "William of Auvergne on the Eternity of the World," *TMS* 68 (1990) 187-205, for William's rejection of the position of some who held that Aristotle did not hold the eternity of the world.

81. In place of the preceding paragraph w has only the following: But if someone says that a certain activity of it has an end, I say that, just as a certain revolution has an end, while all of them are endless and are derived from a power of endless might, so it is in the case at hand. And thus the act itself of understanding is endless without qualification.

<and comes to rest> where there is the continuity of unfailing life, <and no approach to death and failure, no access for sufferings or injuries.> – But if it shall once have attained this end, it is impossible that it be separated from it thereafter. <This is clear from the fact that it is impossible that it be moved by nature to any contrary.> For it is impossible that something be moved naturally from its place; otherwise, <it would neither naturally be moved to that place nor naturally come to rest in it, and thus it would not be its natural place. For the following would happen to it:> it would <naturally> have <two> contrary motions and, hence, <two> contrary natures, <since it is impossible that one nature be moved to two ends or produce two contrary movements.> The reason is that nature is the source of motion and of rest.[82] – But who does not see that it is impossible that it be willingly separated from the very source of life and joy and glory, indeed from the complete fullness of all its desires? – It is impossible that it be violently torn away, because violence can have no place there. For when it has been wholly taken up from itself and from other things which are below it, as from two worlds here below, one higher and the other lower, and has somehow moved into the source of all goods, that is, when that source has wholly taken it up into itself, that [38] is, has gathered *and drawn* all its thoughts into itself <and> all its affections into itself, it lives wholly for it and lives wholly in dependence upon it. This is clearly seen from an example of natural love where the mind of a most loving father lives wholly for his son, and love has wholly turned all thoughts and affections and even external activities toward the son, and he lives his interior life wholly in dependence upon him, since he draws from him all that he thinks and enjoys and fears, and he draws in general from him all his thoughts and affections and finally pours them back upon him. Thus it is in the life of beatitude, because, when the mind is wholly caught up in God and removed from all other things, it will draw its whole life from him alone and will pour it all back and return it to him, because life consists wholly in apprehensions and affections.

---

82. Aristotle, *De caelo* I, 2, 268b11: "We have said that nature is the principle of motion for [natural bodies and magnitudes]." Cf. also *Physics* II, 1, 192b21.

Bibliography

Primary Sources

William of Auvergne. *Guilelmi Alverni Episcopi Parisiensis Opera Omnia.* 2 vols. Edited by F. Hotot, with *Supplementum*, edited by Blaise Le Feron. Orléans-Paris, 1674; repr. Frankfurt a. M., 1963.

_____. *De immortalitate animae.* Edited by Georg Bülow, in *Des Dominicus Gundissalinus Schrift von der Unsterblichkeit der Seele nebst einem Anhange, enthaltend die Abhandlung des Wilhelm von Paris (Auvergne)* De immortalitate animae. In *Beiträge zur Geschichte der Philosophie des Mittelalters* II 3. Münster: Aschendorff, 1897.

_____. *De trinitate.* An Edition of the Latin Text with an Introduction by Bruno Switalski. Toronto: Pontifical Institute of Mediaeval Studies, 1976.

_____. *The Trinity, or the First Principle.* Translated by Francis C. Wade, S.J. and Roland J. Teske, S.J.; introduction and notes by Roland J. Teske, S.J. Milwaukee: Marquette University Press, 1989.

_____. "Tractatus Magistri Guilielmi Alvernensis de bono et malo." Edited by J. Reginald O'Donnell. *MS* 8 (1946) 245-299.

_____. "Tractatus Secundus Guillielmi Alvernensis de bono et malo." Edited by J. Reginald O'Donnell. *MS* 16 (1954) 219-271.

_____. "De arte predicandi. Un manuel de prédication médiévale," *Revue néoscholatique de philosophie* (1923) 192-209.

Secondary Sources

Books

Algazali. *Liber philosophiae.* Edited by Petrus Liechtensteyn. Venice, 1506.

Aristotle. *The Basic Writings of Aristotle*. Edited with an Introduction by Richard McKeon. New York: Random House, 1941.

_____. *Opera*. Edited by I. Bekker. 5 vols. Berlin, 1831-1870.

Augustine of Hippo. *De Genesi ad litteram*. *BA* 48 and 49.

_____. *De trinitate*. *CC* L and La.

Avicebron. *Avencebrolis Fons Vitae*. Ex arabico in latinum translatus ab Johanne Hispano et Dominico Gundissalino. Edited by Clemens Baeumker. In *Beiträge zur Geschichte der Philosophie des Mittelalters* I. Münster: Aschendorff, 1892-1895.

Avicenna. *Avicenna Latinus: Liber de Anima seu Sextus de Naturalibus*. Edition critique de la traduction latine médiévale par Simone van Riet. Introduction sur la doctrine psychologique d'Avicenne par Gerard Verbeke. 2 vols. Louvain: E. Peeters; Leiden: E. J. Brill, 1973 and Louvain: Editions Orientalists; Leiden: E. J. Brill, 1968.

_____. *Avicenna Latinus: Liber de Philosophia Prima sive Scientia Divina*. Edition critique de la traduction latine médievale par Simone van Riet. Introduction doctrinale par Gerard Verbeke. 3 vols. Louvain-La-Neuve: E. Peeters; Leiden: E. J. Brill, 1977, 1983, 1983.

_____. *Le livre de science: I. Logique, métaphysique*. Translated by Mohammed Achena and Henri Massé. Paris: Belles Lettres, 1955.

Borok, Helmut. *Der Tugendbegriff des Wilhelm von Auvergne (1180-1249)*. *Eine moralhistorische Untersuchung zur ideengeschichtliche Rezeption der aristotelischen Ethik*. Düsseldorf: Patmos-Verlag, 1979.

Chenu, M.-D. *Toward Understanding Saint Thomas*. Translated by A.-M. Landy and D. Hughes. Chicago: Regnery, 1964.

Gilson, Etienne. *Elements of Christian Philosophy*. Garden City, N.Y.: Doubleday, 1960.

_____. *History of Christian Philosophy in the Middle Ages*. New York: Random House, 1955.

Glorieux, P. *Répertoire des maîtres en théologie de Paris au xiiie siècle*. Paris: J. Vrin, 1933.

Gregory the Great. *Dialogi de vita et miraculis patrum Italicorum*. *PL* LXXVII,149-430.

_____. *Les dialogues*. *SC* 251, 260, 265. Paris: Editions du Cerf, 1978, 1979, 1980.

Gundissalinus, Dominicus. *De anima*. Edited by J. T. Muckle. *MS* 2 (1949) 23-103.

_____. *De divisione philosophiae*. Edited by L. Baur. In *Beiträge zur Geschichte der Philosophie des Mittelalters* IV 2/3. Münster: Aschendorff, 1903.

_____. *De processione mundi*. Edited by G. Bülow. In *Beiträge zur Geschichte der Philosophie des Mittelalters* XXIV 3. Münster: Aschendorff, 1925.

_____. *De unitate*. Edited by P. Correns. In *Beiträge zur der Philosophie des Mittelalters* I 1. Münster: Aschendorff, 1891.

Klubertanz, George. *The Discursive Power: Sources and Doctrine of the* Vis Cogitativa *According to St. Thomas Aquinas*. St. Louis: The Modern Schoolman, 1952.

Kretzmann, Norman and Anthony Kenny and Jan Pinborg, eds. *The Cambridge History of Later Medieval Philosophy from the Rediscovery of Aristotle to the Disintegration of Scholasticism* 1100-1600. Cambridge: Cambridge University Press, 1982.

Lingenheim, J. *L'art de prier de Guillaume d'Auvergne*. Lyons, 1934.

Lottin, Odon. *Psychologie et Morale aux XIIième et XIIIième Siècles*. 2 vols; 2nd ed. Gembloux: J. Duculot, 1957.

Lubac, Henri de. *The Mystery of the Supernatural*. New York: Herder and Herder, 1965.

Marrone, Steven P. *William of Auvergne and Robert Grosseteste. New Ideas of Truth in the Early Thirteenth Century*. Princeton: Princeton University Press, 1983.

Masnovo, Amato. *Da Guglielmo d'Auvergne a S. Tommaso d'Aquino*. 3 vols; 2nd ed. Milan: Vita et Pensiero, 1946.

Maurer, Armand A. *Medieval Philosophy*. New York: Random House, 1962.

Quentin, Albrecht. *Naturkenntnisse und Naturanschauungen bei Wilhelm von Auvergne*. Hildesheim: Gerstenberg, 1976.

Plato. *Platonis Opera*. Edited by J. Burnett. 5 vols. Oxford, 1899-1906.

_____. *The Dialogues of Plato*. Translated by B. Jowett with an Introduction by Raphael Demos. 2 vols. New York: Random House, 1937.

Plotinus. *Plotini Opera*. Edited by Paul Henry and Hans-Rudolph Schwyzer. 3 vols. Oxford: Oxford University Press, 1962-82.

_____. *Plotinus*. With an English translation by A. H. Armstrong. 6 vols. Cambridge: Harvard University Press, 1966-1988.

Rehm, Bernhard, ed. *Die Pseudoklementinen* II. *Rekognitionen in Rufins Ubersetzung*. Berlin: Akademie Verlag, 1965.

Rohls, Jan. *Wilhelm von Auvergne und der mittelalterliche Aristotelismus*. München: Chr. Kaiser, 1980.

Schindele, Stephan. *Beiträge zur Metaphysik des Wilhelm von Auvergne*. Munich, 1900.

Thomas Aquinas. *Basic Writings of Saint Thomas Aquinas*. Edited and Annotated, with an Introduction by Anton C. Pegis. 2 vols. New York: Random House, 1945.

_____. *Expositio super librum Boethii de trinitate*. Edited by B. Decker. Leiden: Brill, 1955.

_____. *Le "De ente et essentia" de s. Thomas d'Aquin*. Texte établi d'après les manuscrits parisiens. Introduction, notes et études historiques par M.-D. Roland-Gosselin. Paris: J. Vrin, 1948.

_____. *The Division and Methods of the Sciences*. Translated by A. Maurer. Toronto: Pontifical Institute of Mediaeval Studies, 1953.

_____. *On Being and Essence*. Translated with an Introduction and Notes by Armand Maurer. 2nd ed. Toronto: Pontifical Institute of Mediaeval Studies, 1968.

_____. *Opera Omnia*. 24 vols. Parma: P. Fiaccadori, 1852-1873; reprinted New York: Musurgia, 1948-1950.

_____. *Opera Omnia*. Leonine Edition. 27 Vols. Rome: 1882-1985.

Valois, Noël. *Guillaume d'Auvergne, évêque de Paris (1228-1249): Sa vie et ses ouvrages*. Paris: Picard, 1880.

Vaux, Roland de. *Notes et textes sur l'avicennisme latin aux confins des XIIe-XIIIe Siècles*. Paris: J. Vrin, 1934.

Articles

Allard, Baudoin C. "Additions au *Répertoire des maîtres en théologie de Paris au XIIe siècle*," *Bulletin de la société internationale pour l'étude de la philosophie médiévale* 5 (1963) 147-149.

_____. "Note sur le *De immortalitate animae* de Guilaume d'Auvergne," *Bulletin de philosophie médiévale* 18 (1976) 68-72.

_____. "Nouvelles additions et corrections au *Répertoire* de Glorieux: A propos de Guillaume d'Auvergne," *Bulletin de philosophie médiévale* (Louvain) 10-12 (1968-70) 79-80.

Anciaux, P. "Le sacrament de pénitence chez Guillaume d'Auvergne," *Ephemerides Theologicae Lovanienses* 24 (1948) 98-118.

Aubert, R. "Gundissalvi (Dominique), Gundissalinus, Gondisalvi," *Dictionnaire d'histoire et de géographie ecclésiastique*. Vol. 22, pp. 1168-1170. Paris: Letouzey et Ané, 1988.

Baeumker, Clemens. "Dominicus Gundissalinus als philosophischer Schriftsteller," *Compte rendu du 4e congrès scientifique international des catholiques*. IIIe section. Freibourg en Suisse, 1898, pp. 50ff.

Bernstein, Alan E. "Esoteric Theology: William of Auvergne on the Fires of Hell and Purgatory," *Speculum* 57 (1982) 509-531.

_____. "Theology between Heresy and Folkfore: William of Auvergne on Punishment after Death," *Studies in Medieval and Renaissance History* 5 (1982) 4-44.

Chapman, John. "Clementines," *The Catholic Encyclopedia*. 15 vols. New York: Robert Appleton, 1907-1912. Vol. 4, pp. 39-44.

Chenu, M.-D. "Les 'philosophes' dans la philosophie chrétienne médiévale," *Revue des sciences philosophiques et théologiques* 26 (1937) 27-40.

Contenson, P.-M., de. "La théologie de la vision de Dieu au début du XIIIième siècle. Le 'de retributione sanctorum' de Guillaume d'Auvergne et la condamnation de 1241," *Revue de sciences philosophiques et théologiques* 46 (1962) 409-444.

Corti, Guglielmo. "Le sette parte del *Magisterium divinale et sapientiale* di Guglielmo di Auvergne." In *Studi e richerche di scienze religiose in onore dei santi apostoli Petro e Paulo nel XIX centenario del loro martirio*. Romae: Facultas Theologica Pontificae Universitatis Lateranensis, 1968, pp. 289-307.

Davis, Leo. "Creation according to William of Auvergne." In *Studies in Mediaevalia and Americana*. Edited by G. Steckler and L. Davis. Spokane: Gonzaga University Press, 1973, pp. 51-75.

Forest, Aimé. "Guillaume d'Auvergne, critique d'Aristote." In *Etudes médiévales offertes à Augustin Flictie*. Paris: Presses Universitaires de France, 1952, pp. 67-79.

Gauthier, René A. "Notes sur le début du prémier 'averroisme'," *Revue des sciences philosophiques et théologiques* 66 (1982) 321-374.

Gilson, Etienne. "Avicenne en occident au moyen âge," *AHDLMA* 44 (1969) 89-121.

_____. "La notion d'existence chez Guillaume d'Auvergne," *AHDLMA* 21 (1946) 55-91.

_____. "Les 'Philosophantes'," *AHDLMA* 19 (1952) 135-140.

_____. "Les sources gréco-arabes de l'augustinisme avicennisant," *AHDLMA* 4 (1929) 5-149.

_____. "Pourquoi saint Thomas a critiqué saint Augustin," *AHDLMA* 1 (1926) 5-127.

Glorieux, Palemon. "Le tractatus de poenitentia de Guillaume d'Auvergne," *Miscellanea Moralia*. Bibliotheca Ephemeriarum Theologicarum Lovaniensium. Series 1, vols. 2 and 3. Louvain: Nauwelaerts, 1949.

Heinzmann, Richard. "Wilhelm von Auvergne," *Lexikon für Theologie und Kirche*. 2nd ed. Freiburg in Breisgau: Herder, 1965. Vol. 10, p. 1127f.

_____. "Zur Anthropologie des Wilhelm von Auvergne," *Münchener Theologische Zeitschrift* 16 (1965) 27-36.

Jüssen, Gabriel. "Wilhelm von Auvergne." In *Contemporary Philosophy. A New Survey. Volume 6: Philosophy and Science in the Middle Ages*. Part 1. Dordrecht: Kluwer Academic Publishers, 1990, pp. 177-185.

_____. "Wilhelm von Auvergne und die Philosophie im Übergang zur Hochscholastik." In *Thomas von Aquin im philosophischen Gespräch*. Ed. Wolfgang Kluxen. Freiburg and Munich, 1975, pp. 185-203.

Knowles, David. "William of Auvergne," *The Encyclopedia of Philosophy*. 8 vols. New York: Macmillan, 1967. Vol. 8, p. 302f.

Kramp, Josef. "Des Wilhelm von Auverge 'Magisterium Divinale'," *Gregorianum* 1 (1920) 538-613, 2 (1921) 42-103 and 174-195.

Landgraf, A. "Der Tracktat de 'De errore Pelagii' des Wilhelm von Auvergne," *Speculum* 5 (1930) 168-180.

_____. "Wilhelm von Auvergne," *Lexicon für Theologie und Kirche*. Vol. 10 (1938), pp. 890-891.

Lindberg, David C. "The Transmission of Greek and Arabic Learning to the West." In *Science in the Middle Ages*. Edited by David C. Lindberg. Chicago: University of Chicago Press, 1978, pp. 52-90.

Longpré, Ephrem. "Guillaume d'Auvergne et Alexandre de Halès," *Archivum Franciscanum Historicum* 16 (1923) 249-250.

_____. "Guillaume d'Auvergne et l'Ecole Franciscaine de Paris," *La France Franciscaine* 5 (1922) 426-429.

Maréchal, Joseph. "La notion d'extase, d'après l'enseignement traditionel des mystiques et des théologiens," *Nouvelle revue théologique* 64 (1937) 986-998.

Masnovo, Amato. "Guglielmo d'Auvergne e l'universita di Parigi dal 1229 al 1231." In *Melanges Mandonnet* II. Paris: Librairie J. Vrin, 1930, pp. 191-232.

Michaud-Quantin, P. and M. Lemoine. "Pour le dossier des 'philosophantes'," *AHDLMA* 35 (1968) 17-22.

Moody, Ernest A. "William of Auvergne and his Treatise De Anima," *Studies in Medieval Philosophy, Science, and Logic*. Berkeley and Los Angeles: The University of California Press, 1975, pp. 1-109.

O'Donnell, J. Reginald. "The Notion of Being in William of Auvergne," *Proceedings of the American Catholic Philosophical Association* 21 (1946) 156-165.

_____. "The *Rhetorica Divina* of William of Auvergne. A Study in Applied Rhetoric." In *Images of Man in Ancient and Medieval Thought*. Leuven: Leuven Univ. Press, 1976, pp. 323-333.

_____. "William of Auvergne (of Paris)," *The New Catholic Encyclopedia*. 15 vols. New York: McGraw-Hill, 1967. Vol. 14, p. 921.

Smalley, Beryl. "William of Auvergne, John of La Rochelle and Saint Thomas on the Old Law." In *St. Thomas Aquinas 1274-1974 Commemorative Studies*, II. Toronto: Pontifical Institute of Medieval Studies, 1974, pp. 11-71.

Teske, Roland J. "The Identity of the *Italici* in William of Auvergne's Discussion of the Eternity of the World," *Proceedings of the PMR Conference* 15 (1990), 191-203.

_____. "William of Auvergne on the Eternity of the World," *TMS* 67 (1990) 187-205.

_____. "William of Auvergne's Rejection of the Agent Intellect." In *Supportive – Confrontation: Greek and Medieval Studies in Honor of Leo Sweeney, S.J.* (New York: Peter Lang, 1992), forthcoming.

Vanneste, A. "Nature et grâce dans la théologie de Guillaume d'Auxerre et de Guillaume d'Auvergne," *Ephemerides Theologicae Lovanienses* 3 (1977) 83-106.

Vaux, Roland de. "La première entrée d'Averroës chez les Latins," *Revue de sciences philosophiques et théologiques* 22 (1933) 193-245.

Vernet, F. "Guillaume d'Auvergne, évêque de Paris," *Dictionnaire de théologie catholique*. Vol. VII, 1967-1976.

Viard, P. "Guillaume d'Auvergne," *Dictionnaire de spiritualité* 6 (1967) 1182-1192.

Wulf, M. de. *Histoire de la philosophie médiévale. VI, 2. Le treizième siècle*. Louvain: Institut supérieur de philosophie, 1936.

Index of Names

Index of Terms

MARQUETTE UNIVERSITY PRESS

Mediaeval Philosophical Texts in Translation

Published by: Marquette University Press, Marquette University, Milwaukee, WI 53233. **Manuscript submissions should be sent to:** Chair, MPTT Editorial Board, Dept. of Philosophy, Coughlin Hall, Marquette University, Milwaukee, WI 53233.